Praise for Sarah Intelligator
Live, Laugh, Find True Love

"In over thirty years of therapy with couples, helping many of them try to make a relationship work that they probably shouldn't have been in to begin with, I have seen but not put labels to the patterns that Sarah Intelligator describes in her excellent book *Live, Laugh, Find True Love*. What she helps readers with is spot-on, and while it's true when she writes that 'you won't like what you are about to read,' the book will nonetheless save readers many years of pain and disappointment. This book should be required reading for anyone looking to date or consider a committed relationship, to go in with eyes open and a clear mind."

—Dr. Sarah Salzman (formerly, Dr. Sarah Rattray), founder
of the Couples Communication Institute and certified
Gottman Institute couples and relationship counselor

"Sarah has the gift of giving comforting, wise, holistic advice that empowers and brings a much-needed hope to the relationship journey."

—Caitlin Crosby, singer, songwriter, actress, TedX speaker,
founder of the Giving Keys, and an *Oprah* SuperSoul100
visionary and influential leader

"Everyone looking for their 'person' (or looking for love) should read this book. It's packed with inspirational and life-changing content to ensure you will never settle again and shows that you deserve a healthy and happy relationship, and Sarah helps you get there! . . . This book is about knowing what's best for you and sticking with it. It is empowering, inspirational, and packed with powerful tools to help you on your journey to a healthy, fun, fulfilling, and forever relationship. Sarah teaches you how to trust yourself and your intuition which, to me, is the most priceless gift you can give yourself."

—Jaime Bronstein, LCSW, author of *MAN*ifesting: A Step-By-Step Guide to Attracting the Love That Is Meant for You* and host of *Love Talk Live*

"As a couples therapist, these six 'F Words' are keys to learning about yourself on so many levels to be able to be not just successful in your relationships, but thrive for many years with depth, love, and fulfillment. . . . This book is inspiring, insightful, and in your face with truth and realness from an amazing perspective and behind the scenes viewpoint of the ugliness of relationships to help shine a light on the beauty of what a relationship can be."

—Eli Weinstein, LCSW, private practice therapist

"As a certified divorce & relationship decision coach, I encounter the aftermath of crumbling marriages daily. This book, presented through Sarah Intelligator's discerning lens as a divorce attorney, is a beacon of hope for struggling couples. Packed with invaluable insights and wisdom, it serves as a lifeline to keep relationships alive and thriving in the midst of struggle. It reframes how couples can navigate challenges by identifying and breaking unhealthy patterns that get in the way of establishing and maintaining a healthy connection. If you're on the brink of marital breakdown or seeking to find lasting love, prepare to be enlightened and transformed!"

—Cindy Stibbard, certified divorce & relationship decision coach, founder of Divorce ReDefined, host of *Divorce ReDefined: Changing the Experience of Divorce* podcast

LIVE, LAUGH, FIND TRUE LOVE

**A Step-By-Step Guide to Finding
a Meaningful Relationship**

SARAH INTELLIGATOR, ESQ.

A DIVORCE ATTORNEY!

Foreword by Dr. Sarah Salzman
Introductions by Caitlin Crosby & Kelly Kruger Brooks

Skyhorse Publishing

Skyhorse Publishing books may be purchased in bulk at special discounts for sales promotion, corporate gifts, fund-raising, or educational purposes. Special editions can also be created to specifications. For details, contact the Special Sales Department, Skyhorse Publishing, 307 West 36th Street, 11th Floor, New York, NY 10018 or info@skyhorsepublishing.com.

Skyhorse® and Skyhorse Publishing® are registered trademarks of Skyhorse Publishing, Inc.®, a Delaware corporation.

Visit our website at www.skyhorsepublishing.com.

10 9 8 7 6 5 4 3 2 1

Library of Congress Cataloging-in-Publication Data is available on file.

Cover design by David Ter-Avanesyan
Cover images: Getty Images
Edited by Nicole Frail and Catherine Miller

Print ISBN: 978-1-5107-7640-1
Ebook ISBN: 978-1-5107-7641-8

Printed in the United States of America

Dedicated to my husband, Joel Warsh, without whom I would have continued to procrastinate and never actually written (or finished) this book.

And to my mom, who invested countless hours painstakingly helping me hone my writing skills.

CONTENTS

Foreword
by Dr. Sarah Salzman
Founder of the
Couples Communication Institute

"Hindsight is 20/20"

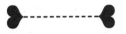

You know the feeling. You get to the end of the story, and knowing how it ended, you wish you could go back to the beginning and do it differently.

In my thirty-five years as a leading couples psychologist, I saw couples in pain from distance, conflict, betrayal, and disappointment finally willing to do what they could to repair.

I was committed to helping whoever was ready to rekindle their struggling relationship, and I listened closely to the stories every couple shared of their histories from the time that they first met. They often revealed not only the fundamental mismatches that were there from the beginning, but also the absence of clear communication right from the start. So rarely did couples honestly and plainly explore themselves, each other, and what being in a long-term relationship with each other might actually be like. From where we were all sitting when they were in my office, it was like they were getting to the end of their story, and—knowing how it unfolded—wishing they could go back to the beginning and do it differently.

Sarah Intelligator writes that "a fulfilling relationship not only enhances your own life, but it serves as a bona fide Butterfly Effect, promulgating a far-reaching impact on the world around you." That is essentially my mission with couples—to help them support each other so they can make a difference in their world. In my practice, and in the Couples Communication Institute where I am Founder and CEO, I teach the central importance of healthy communication for people already in a relationship, who sometimes see learning to communicate as a last resort. Sarah's book brings home the importance of open, curious, honest communication and self-assessment from the very start. Imagine how much easier it is to achieve a fulfilling relationship when you start out with the right partner, one you're so much more likely to stay with forever.

When Sarah Intelligator first shared with me the book she was writing, based on her career as a divorce attorney, my eyes grew wide with excitement at the "20/20 hindsight" power in her hands that she was conjuring. Having been divorced myself, I found myself nodding in agreement and saying "YES!" while recognizing myself and my clients page after page.

One of the things I teach every person I ever work with: you can want what you want. You deserve to listen to yourself. You are worth standing up and saying, "This is, or isn't, right for me." Whereas I tend to teach this to people many years down the road, Sarah is here to tell you that you can, and should, respect what you know to be true about yourself from the very start. She has heard what I have heard: one version or another of "I knew this wasn't right for me in the beginning, but I didn't know I could stand in my power and own it." That's the thing about red flags—when you see them, you ignore them at your peril.

While therapists tend to help fix, mend, and heal, attorneys tend to get you out of the mess you've made, or warn and prepare you in advance to not get into a mess to begin with.

Having spent her career helping people divorce their way out of the relationship mess they've gotten into, Sarah is now sharing with you how you can avoid your own personal future mess. Listen to her—she knows what she's talking about.

Because, which would you really, truly rather do:

1) Commit to a relationship now, only for it to end in disappointment and heartbreak years in the future, never being able to relive and reclaim those lost years, or

2) Take your time now to be a little more careful, with your eyes open, and do the work to find the relationship that you can sustain together for a lifetime?

If you chose 2) then this book is for you.

Sarah Intelligator's brilliant and entertaining "Live, Laugh, Find True Love" walks you through what you need to do to open your eyes, how to be careful, and outlines the work it takes. You will learn the six "F-word" categories you deserve to, and in fact need to, explore within yourself and with your dating partners, to set yourselves up for a successful and happy relationship and not a painful divorce. Sarah pushes you to honor and respect the importance of each category, and warns you not to "yes, but" yourself out of paying attention to the red flags that are waving right in front of you.

Entering a relationship with the hope that your partner will change, or the belief that you will be the magic person to help them finally change, is folly. Sarah Intelligator's depth of experience reveals what last-ditch efforts can't fix . . . and how to avoid getting into the position to begin with.

Her tough-love approach pulls no punches, and her belief in the necessity of brutal honesty from her to you comes through in the whole book. She's not your friend trying to gently dance around pointing out warning signs. If you want to hear it straight, Sarah will tell it to you straight. When you know your future is at stake, this is tremendously valuable.

One of my favorite categories Sarah covers is "Fundamental Values." In therapy I spend a great deal of time with couples, helping them unbury their unspoken or disregarded Fundamental Values. Sarah flips this around and makes clear the importance of figuring out and discussing your values with each other from the very beginning. A powerful exercise guides you to look ahead at where you see yourself in each decade of your life, into the future. Too many couples enjoy each other at the time they meet, and want that exact feeling to continue forever, without exploring what they believe they will want as time goes by. For example, while you're dating you may enjoy the way you spend your weekends together, but . . . how do you want to spend your weekends in a few years, when you're building your careers; when you have babies, small children, teenagers; when your children leave the nest; when you retire? Are these visions compatible at all? Believe me, I have seen the years of pain in couples where one person assumed and expected they'd get to golf every weekend forever, while the other assumed and expected full partnership with children's weekend sports, activities, and enrichment. Bitter fights and stony silences could have been avoided with introspection and clear communication in the beginning.

Pay close attention to the "Fear" category, as Sarah so clearly explores the power that Fear exerts to make you ignore all the other red flags. Yes, you may be afraid that time is running out for a perfect partner, so you might believe the time is now to settle for the one in front of you. But are you really, truly ready to commit with your eyes closed, only to end the relationship in a few years' time, having missed your opportunity for someone with whom you really are compatible?

This book should be required reading for anyone looking to date or considering a committed relationship, allowing them to go in with eyes open and a clear mind. Sarah holds your feet to the fire to pay attention to all the F-Words, to protect you when you're tempted to not protect yourself . . . as any good attorney should!

INTRODUCTION
by Caitlin Crosby
Founder & CEO of The Giving Keys

I'd love to introduce you to a force of nature. Her name is Sarah Intelligator. This colorful, wise, strong woman serendipitously burst into my life at just the right time.

I first met her through her husband who is our family's pediatrician, Dr. Joel Warsh. I remember walking into his office and thinking he had the most high quality, tasteful decor for a children's doctor's office. He told me that although his wife was a family law and divorce attorney, she also did the interior decorations for his office. Then I met her in the flesh at a farmers market and saw the powerful, dynamic, masterpiece that she was.

I have since been going through my own divorce and know how painful it can be. The guidance that she gave me through the process, and in this book, gave me the tools to both emotionally (and lawfully) fight the good fight as well as help me select the right partner this time around.

When everything started to fall apart, I knew I needed some legal counsel, and she was the first person who came to mind. My father and I sat down for lunch with her and were both so impressed with her expertise and knowledge. Not only did she give me clear next steps, but she also empathized with me as a human being and peppered in marriage and relationship wisdom I needed to be reminded of.

1

Hearing from someone like her who sees things from her very specific perspective gave me clear insight. To hear all the stories and patterns that lead to the demise of a marriage taught me what it takes to choose wisely which leads to making it work. Sarah's background and how it plays into her book is unique to other dating and relationship books as she sees things through the back door, from behind the curtain.

In my previous relationship, we did a bit of premarital counseling, but they didn't ask a lot of the questions Sarah is bringing to light in her book. I love her nonemotional, rational and objective questions. I also love her "why": that part of having a meaningful life is finding a partner who will push you to be the best version of yourself.

The reader will learn to ask the strategic questions, watch for the green and red flags, and discover what it takes to disrupt the downward trend of divorce statistics and unsuccessful marriages. She's the right person for the job; she's able to teach you the tricks and blind spots she's discovered. She's discovered them through a lens of working backwards, deducting what formulas do and don't work. Her "Five Pillars" are brilliant. It's so helpful to see them laid out and communicated so clearly. Doing the exercises and journal prompts asking yourself the fundamentally important questions were so eye opening. Not only are we asking ourselves the hard questions, but she prepares us to ask the hard questions to potential partners we are considering. The steps and findings teach us how to avoid these predictable patterns in our current and future relationships.

In this day and age, I believe some of our generation get polluted with how films (and God forbid, reality television) depict relationships. That becomes our norm, our gauge. Thankfully Sarah reminds us of HEALTHY love. That it takes: Trust, Honesty, Communication, Teamwork and Respect.

Not only is she a divorce attorney with over twenty years of experience that most relationship experts don't have, but she's also been through her own divorce, so she can truly relate with empathy and grace. This book is for every type of person looking to find and keep a long-term relationship. Her cut and dry, no-nonsense approach will surely point you in the right direction.

Not only did she help me understand all the NOT fun legal realities, but we also became friends, and her holistic advice helped me the entire way. Everything from finally separating my bank account and leaving the bank, receiving empowering memes of Angela Bassett walking away from a burning car to remind me of the powerful fire inside me to have the strength to face all these things, and of course creating healthy boundaries for myself and children. Her lines of wisdom to share with my children helped them cope, understand, and heal. Things like, "Your dad and I had different ideas of what it means to be married."

The proof that her heart is in the right place is that she's trying to put herself out of a job. She doesn't want more families to walk into her office. I greatly respect that she's now focusing on helping more people not find themselves in that wasteful, painful predicament. She's done the work and is doing the work so we can learn from the very best. I know you will not only enjoy, but have a happier, healthier life because of it!

INTRODUCTION
by Kelly Kruger Brooks

As an actress, especially a soap actress, I would say I know a thing or two about tumultuous relationships and what not to do! Both from characters I've played on-screen, friends I have comforted throughout the years, and as someone who has experienced my own highs and lows of love, I wholeheartedly recommend this book and believe that it has the power to transform your relationships. Sarah, a successful divorce attorney, has poured her heart and soul into this work, skillfully weaving her professional knowledge with her personal experiences to create a compelling and insightful guide to love and marriage.

Many people don't know that I was married before. I had been married at the young age of eighteen, and by the time I turned twenty-seven, I was facing the harsh reality of divorce. I searched for comfort in many books, and I truly feel this is exactly the book I needed. Fortunately, I found love again and unknowingly applied so many of these principles, which is why I believe my marriage is successful today.

While reading this book, I came to fully understand the factors that contributed to the failure of my relationship and why these were so important to consider in my current one. I was able to identify the "F-words" that Sarah so eloquently describes in this book: Fundamental Values, Foundation, Family, Fixing, Fairy Tale, and Fear.

By understanding these factors and applying the lessons I learned from my friend Sarah, my marriage has become even more solid than it was before.

As an actress, I have had the privilege of portraying characters from all walks of life, each with their own trials and tribulations. This unique perspective has given me the ability to empathize with others more, as I have come to understand that the journey of love and relationships is a universal one. No matter who you are or where you come from, the desire to love and be loved is something that unites us all.

That is why I believe that this book is so important. Sarah's intimate understanding of the intricacies of relationships combined with her professional expertise as a divorce attorney make her the perfect person to guide you on your own journey toward a fulfilling and lasting relationship.

From the first page to the last, this book is filled with wisdom, compassion, and the kind of practical advice that can only come from someone who has truly walked the walk. Whether you are single, married, or somewhere in between, this book will provide you with invaluable insights into the world of love and relationships.

So, if you are looking to strengthen your relationship, heal from a breakup, or simply gain a deeper understanding of the complexities of love, I wholeheartedly recommend this book. By sharing her experiences and expertise, my dear friend has created a valuable resource that has the potential to change your life for the better.

Together, let us embark on a journey of self-discovery, growth, and, ultimately, the kind of love that will stand the test of time. With the guidance of this book and the wisdom of its author, I am confident that you, too, can find the love you deserve.

Chapter 1
An Introduction to Relationsh*ts

"If you don't know where you are going, any road will
get you there." —Lewis Carroll

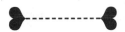

You won't like what you are about to read. I am going to tell you what you already know but are too scared to admit. I am going to tell you what your friends say about your relationship choices behind your back but won't say to your face. It will upset you. You will be uncomfortable. Then again, if you didn't want to hear it, you wouldn't have picked up this book.

In the United States, approximately 50 percent of marriages end in divorce. Of the 50 percent, almost 100 percent of those marriages *should never have existed* in the first place. How do I know? Not only am I a divorce attorney, but I myself have been divorced. Let's face it, I'm a veritable expert in relationsh*ts.

In the close to two decades that I have been practicing Family Law, I have seen it all—the good, the bad, your run-of-the mill bevy of sociopaths, narcissists, and everything in between. Yes, I've seen some weird and crazy things. Yet, no matter how weird and crazy, relationships almost always fail for the *same* reasons. While people may choose to end their relationships for various personal reasons, underlying those myriad reasons are ultimately *six* predictable, albeit *avoidable*, patterns. Fifty percent of the population repeats at least one, if not all, of these six identifiable patterns, only to later wonder, "Where did I go wrong?"

It's no mystery. I will tell you precisely where *they* went wrong, so that *you* don't. This book is going to be really bad for business.

I am not here to tell you what you *want* to hear. I am here to tell you what you *need* to hear. Some of you will get defensive. Some of you will read this book and think to yourselves: "That's not me." "I don't do that." "My relationship is perfect!" Surely, these are the comfortable reactions. You convince yourself, "This person is right for me" to validate a relationship you suspect may be wrong. You reassure yourself, "Sarah doesn't know what she's talking about." You insulate yourself from the inevitable pain that will accompany a breakup. Our minds have this amazing way of justifying anything to conveniently fit our neatly packaged narrative. They do this to protect us from feeling hurt and discomfort. Maybe your relationship *is* right. I'm not saying it isn't. All I ask is as you read this book, you remain objective and honest with yourself. Hey, I only stand to gain if you aren't.

People are typically incredulous when their marriages fail. Frankly, I would have been surprised if their marriages succeeded. One need not be a psychic—although, admittedly, my powers of prediction are often so eerily accurate, I genuinely question whether I might be. One must simply recognize the patterns, which I will identify for you in this book in the hope that you, too, will come to recognize and avoid them.

Whether you are divorced and want to remarry, whether you have been in and out of failed relationships, whether you are uncertain about an existing relationship, whether you are prepared to ditch the single life and find a life partner, whether you are gay, trans, nonbinary, straight—whatever your race, gender, religion or sexual preference—this book is for you. By showing you the reasons people get divorced, I will also show you the ways to prevent it. I firmly believe every human being deserves to love and be loved in the *right* way.

Despite living in undeniably divisive times, we are all united by our primal need for companionship. This notion serves as an ever-present reminder that, beneath the semantics and our diverse ideologies, we are all made of the same flesh and bone—driven by identical biological forces. Regardless of one's sexual orientation, political party, gender or gender identity, religion, race or ethnicity, every single *human being* fundamentally wants to love and be loved. How very beautiful that when we distill away the labels, we all want the *same* thing. If we can just learn how to find it, we can experience a meaningful and fulfilling love. And, when we truly feel loved, we lead a more harmonious existence. In turn, this love reverberates into our jobs, our parenting, to our families and friends and into the world. A fulfilling relationship does not only enhance your life. It acts as a bona fide Butterfly Effect, emitting its far-reaching influence on the world around you.

In stark contrast, a tempestuous relationship invariably invites unhappiness and other extreme psychological consequences. While I most certainly do not purport to be an expert in mood disorders, common sense dictates that a turbulent relationship contributes to anxiety, depression, and even suicidal ideations, to which I have watched so many wonderful people succumb. It comes as no surprise to me that, as divorce rates climb, so do the rates of anxiety, depression, and mental health issues. Although unhappy marriages are most certainly *not* the sole reason for the increase in mood disorders and mental health issues, they are, without a doubt, a contributing factor. Quite often, I watch previously unafflicted people grapple with situational depression and anxiety, directly stemming from the inexorable struggles in their relationships. When divorce is the only plausible way out, people feel imprisoned by their relationship. Understandably, they do everything to avoid the unmentionable "D" word. They feel trapped, exacerbating their despair, and fueling a self-perpetuating cycle of hopelessness.

You, dear reader, would not be the first to note my flair for hyperbole. Yet, I assure you. This scenario is all too real and sadly prevalent.

I am not trying to scare you, but you should be at least a little bit scared. Relationships are not the bogieman. You shouldn't fear *them*. You should be afraid of the *wrong* relationship. Given the potential consequences, selecting the wrong relationship may deter you from forming *any* relationship. No need to panic and embrace the single life forever, though. In writing this book, my aim is to show you the ways to discern between the right and wrong relationships. I will peel back the curtain, giving you VIP backstage access to the inner workings of human relationships—the gritty stuff the audience doesn't typically get to see.

Sometimes, I wish I could take couples on a divorce field trip before they get married—you know, let them sit in on my contentious calls with opposing counsel or meetings with frantic clients. I'd love nothing more than for these soon-to-be newlywed lovebirds to observe a Family Law trial or a hearing. Maybe they could watch mothers and fathers run out of the courtroom sobbing hysterically after the judge awards what they believe to be too much custody to the other parent. Perhaps these wide-eyed sweethearts could read some of the snarky emails flung back and forth between two people who, at one time, were madly in love. The emails can be downright nasty and deeply hurtful. Or possibly, they might observe how very tedious it is to produce several years' worth of bank, credit card, and various other statements, in response to an onerous demand for production of documents.

I wouldn't enjoy taking you on this little field trip. After all, I'm not a sadist. Far from it. I simply think that, nay, I *know*, when you are so focused on picking the perfect table linens or bridesmaid dresses, you are not thinking about what is truly important. I hate to break it to you

(I will anyway): mermaid, A-line or ball gown with the most perfect sweetheart pinch do not determine the success of your relationship. The perfect wedding band and caterer may make for an unforgettably epic party, about which your friends will fondly reminisce for years to come. None of that matters when you and your partner are unable to navigate life's tumultuous waters together. If you cannot work as a team to traverse obstacles, you will grow apart and, regrettably, end up sobbing in my office, another statistic. I don't want this for you. More importantly, *you* don't want this for yourself.

I cannot tell you how many clients have said to me, "I wish someone had told me how much easier it is to get married than to get divorced." "If I knew how expensive divorce would be, I never would have gotten married." They lament, "I never would have married him or her if I knew how awful divorce would be." The answer, my friends, is *not* to dodge marriage. It is to marry the *right* person. Steer clear of the patterns that will almost inevitably lead to your divorce. Choosing the right partner has the power to greatly enhance your life. I would hate for you to deprive yourself of a fulfilling and meaningful lifelong relationship because you are avoiding relationships altogether. Rather, I want to provide you with guidelines to help you avoid the wrong partner and find the right one.

Divorce is one of the most excruciatingly painful and financially deleterious experiences a human being can go through. I hope you never step foot in my office. I stand before you, shouting from the highest rooftop, imploring you to hear and heed my words. Why do I do this? Surely I only profit from your decisions. I'll tell you the reason: I care. I know you don't know me, but I really do. I have gone through my own divorce, and I have guided countless good (and some not so good) people through theirs. Plainly put, divorce sucks. I want to stop you from repeating the patterns that you have the power to avoid.

I want you to put in the work *right now* to find a partner with whom you will truly enjoy a fulfilling and meaningful future, even if that means experiencing some pain on your path to getting there. It's called delayed gratification and, trust me, it's worth it.

Your choices in this very moment determine whether you end up crying in my office, squandering your child's college fund, and asking the question, "Where did I go wrong?" I am here to help you change the trajectory of your narrative. I am here to help you find a meaningful and long-lasting relationship. Chinese philosopher Lao Tzu said, "The journey of a thousand miles begins with one step." By picking up this book, you've already taken that first and very important step.

Chapter 2
The "F-Words"

"Learn from the mistakes of others. You can't live long enough to make them all yourself." —Eleanor Roosevelt

Over the years, I have identified certain patterns among virtually all failed relationships. These patterns occur with such frequent regularity that they are predictable—at least, they are to me. My hope is that these patterns will come to be equally obvious to you. If you can learn to recognize these patterns in your own relationship, then, ideally, you will avoid them, and accordingly, avoid the wrong relationship.

No doubt, some will chastise me for "stereotyping." Yet, all examples I give in this book are based on patterns I see over and over again in my practice. Please know, I use prevalent examples not to disparage or stereotype, but to serve the very important didactic function of helping others recognize and elude similar patterns. Think of me like the albatross wrapped tightly around the sailor's neck in Samuel Taylor Coleridge's "Rime of the Ancient Mariner." Like the albatross, I am here to remind you of the burdens and regrets of others.

We all know the meaning of the word "pattern." The Cambridge English dictionary defines "pattern" as a "particular way something usually happens or is done." A pattern is predictable because it repeats over and over again. In the context of relationships, patterns are the repetition of human behaviors—the way most people will predictably act under a similar set of circumstances in their interpersonal relationships. In watching relationships fail, I continuously observe others recapitulate certain behaviors. I monotonously munch away at my popcorn, watching a film I have seen hundreds of times before. I already know how it ends—the plot is always the same. The patterns echoed time and time again invariably lead to divorce. Nonetheless, people continue to repeat them. Yes, these patterns are so apparent to me (as they will become to you) that, without even consulting my crystal ball, I can prognosticate whether a relationship will fail and the reasons it will fail.

I am going to share with you the knowledge I have gleaned from my years of experience as a Family Law attorney, in the hope that you, too, will learn to identify these patterns, and, in doing so, will not succumb to them.

I have broken these patterns down into six simple categories called the "F-Words":

1. **Fundamental values**
2. **Fear**
3. **Foundation**
4. **Fixing**
5. **Fairy tale**
6. **Family**

Throughout this book, we will explore each of these F-Words in great detail. For now, let's start by identifying them and walk through a short introduction to each.

Fundamental Values

Among the most common patterns I encounter in failed relationships is the absence of or dissonant fundamental values. A "value" is one's principle or standard of behavior; one's judgment of what is important in life. We define ourselves by what we deem important. Our fundamental values are so inextricably linked to our identity that, often, they determine the path we take in our lives. We *are* our values. You get the picture. Fundamental values are kind of a big deal. Yet, when our partner's fundamental values differ from or even conflict with our own, we marginalize this not-so-trivial detail in favor of companionship.

We sleep with someone on a first date and only after do we take the time to get to know him or her. Before you fetch your pitchfork, rest assured, I'm not shaming anyone. Far from it. There is nothing wrong with sleeping with someone on a first date. However, it does deprive you of the opportunity to *first* ascertain an indispensable piece of information that will determine whether this relationship has potential. Of course, this person was "so good in bed" that you are now more attached than you would have been had you abstained. Your desire to go on a second date has little to do with whether this person's values align with your own and everything to do with physical attraction. You are officially infatuated. All of this is good and fine if you are looking for a casual hook-up. If you are genuinely seeking a life partner, horny though you may be, it is not advisable. Sleeping with someone on the first date does not mean your relationship will fail. And no, you will not always know on a first or even second date whether you and your partner share fundamental values. When your goal is to find a life partner, the first or second date should be spent trying to determine whether your fundamental values (and not your genitals) align.

At our core, each of us has an average of three to five fundamental values that define our identity, our moral compass, and our outlook on life, so much so that these principles or standards shape the decisions we make and dictate the way we live our lives.

To help you start to identify your own fundamental values, I have compiled a list of a mere few commonly held fundamental values:

- **Organization**
- **Family**
- **Religion/Faith**
- **Politics**
- **Adventure**
- **Spirituality**
- **Education**
- **Tradition**
- **Career**

- **Health**
- **Loyalty**
- **Hobbies/Interests**
- **Wanderlust**
- **Independence**
- **Financial Stability**
- **Friendship**
- **Comfort**
- **Frugality**

I could easily come up with more, as I am sure could you. The point is to provide you with a working list from which you, yourself, may choose three to five that resonate. If you can think of others, great. If you can't identify three to five values from this list, or you cannot think of any on your own, that's perfectly all right. In the next chapter, we will do an exercise that will help you define your own fundamental values. Perhaps you may have identified with three specific values on my list, but, after completing this exercise, you will discover you fundamentally value something you never contemplated.

Why are values, or, more specifically, fundamental values so important that they earn the coveted honor of first F-Word? If fundamental values are your standard of behavior, then it follows that someone whose standard of behavior does not comport with yours is incompatible with you. Of course, this is a gross oversim-plification. Put another way, if values are one's judgment of what is important in life, then he or she should share his or her life with one who deems those *same* things important. If different things are important to you and your partner—more than merely your favorite foods or your favorite band—then you may end up want-ing different things in life. You may want to raise your children differently or impart upon them disparate ideals. This will invari-ably give rise to irreconcilable conflicts in your marriage and, ulti-mately, your divorce.

Many years ago, I represented an Orthodox Jewish woman. After she and her husband were married, she gave birth to a baby boy. The wife (my client) insisted on raising their son in the Orthodox Jewish faith. While the husband was, himself, Jewish and wanted to raise his son in the Jewish faith, he did not believe in the Orthodox Jewish practices. Ultimately, this dissonance in fundamental values led to the breakdown of the relationship. Even within the same faith, the wife's devout beliefs were so divergent from the husband's that the relationship could not withstand this rudimentary difference. During their divorce, the wife attempted to limit the husband's cus-todial time with their son. She did not believe that the husband would keep kosher or observe other Orthodox traditions.

When fundamental values do not align, the relationship cannot succeed. Scenarios like this one make for the ugliest custody battles. You are probably not thinking about what faith, if any, you are going to raise your kids in when the conversation is effortlessly flowing over a bottle of Chardonnay, or you have your tongue down the throat of that hot guy or girl you met on that dating app. *You should be*, though.

Two people may share superficial interests. This does not mean they share fundamental values. Sure, both may have loved to travel, and they may have traveled quite fervently when they were young and relatively free of serious adult responsibilities. When they had a mortgage, careers, two children and could no longer travel like they once did, there was no common thread left holding them together.

That is not to say that the love of travel cannot or should not be one of your fundamental values. This is the reason identifying three to five fundamental values that resonate with *you* is so important. The woman who never wants to have children and wants to travel the world for the rest of her life would best be suited for a similarly nomadic partner who, too, does not care to have children. It is equally important to ascertain whether your interests are fleeting or specific to this current stage of your life, or whether they will forever be essential to your existence. Sure, you may be content selling off all your worldly possessions and traveling the world when you are in your early twenties. You may think you never want to have children. Is this the way you still picture yourself when you are forty or fifty? If you are at least open to the idea of having children, you do not want to choose a partner who is adamantly opposed to having them.

The more fundamental values you and your partner share, the more likely you are to share mutual goals and seek to achieve those goals in the same way. This ensures you will grow together rather than apart. In contrast, when your and your partner's fundamental values are grossly disparate (you are conservative, your partner is liberal; you are content renting for the rest of your life, your partner wants to own property, etc.), this should raise that infamous "red flag," one which, hopefully, will not end up swept under that inviting rug.

In the chapter "What in the F-Word is a Fundamental Value?", you will learn how to identify your fundamental values. We will delve deeper into the reasons shared fundamental values are so indispensable to the longevity of a relationship, and the reasons that, without them, the relationship is likely destined for divorce.

Fear

Fear is the predominant reason most relationships fail. Bold statement. I know. I wouldn't make it if it was not true. Human beings are so terrified at the prospect of being alone, never finding someone else or never finding someone better, that they will, quite literally, settle for things that make them unhappy—things they *know* deep down inside they do not want for the rest of their lives. They mollify their conscience, convincing themselves they can live with characteristics they know are "deal breakers." I rarely hear someone say, "I would rather spend the rest of my life alone than be with someone who doesn't deserve me." Funnily enough, those unwilling to settle typically find their ideal mates. Those content with the wrong mate, or *any* mate, are the ones who end up in my office. They are only delaying the inevitable, while relegating themselves to more pain than they would have experienced had they called it quits when their intuition told them they should.

Of course, relinquishing fear is far easier said than done. Fear is a primal and powerful force. In the chapter "Have No Fear, Your Intelligence Is Here," you will explore ways to transcend your fears. You will learn to use your strength to leave a relationship to which you have been clinging because the prospect of being alone is too terrifying an alternative. You will also learn how to avoid getting involved in the wrong relationship in the first place.

Foundation

Like fundamental values, foundation is indispensable to a successful relationship. Yet, foundation is distinguishable from fundamental values. Whereas one's fundamental values are unique to that particular individual, they *vary* from person to person and from relationship to relationship. However, the characteristics that make up a solid foundation are the *same* in every single relationship. A successful relationship unequivocally requires the presence of all five of the following Pillars:

- **Trust**
- **Honesty**
- **Communication**
- **Teamwork**
- **Respect**

Both partners work together to resolve their shared problems, and they support each other in the face of individual struggles. A successful relationship *cannot* exist unless each of these Five Pillars is present. So many relationships fail because one or all Pillars are absent. In the chapter "The House that 'Foundation' Built," you will explore each Pillar in greater depth. You will understand the reason each Pillar, individually, and all Five Pillars, collectively, are so indispensable to a successful relationship. You will learn how to distinguish between weak and strong Pillars in your own relationship.

Fixing

Have you ever been in a relationship and thought to yourself, "If only this person could _____, then our relationship would be perfect." Sound familiar? There is a difference between mutual growth and fixing. The former is a signpost of a healthy and symbiotic relationship. The latter is quite the contrary.

Let's imagine you are in your kitchen. You're thirsty, so you open the cupboard and reach for a glass. You notice a chip in the rim of the glass or maybe a crack in its side. Do you use this glass, or do you throw it away and get another one? (Please don't drink from chipped glass!)

It's so obvious, right? You toss that broken glass in the trash and get another one, one that won't hurt you. You don't want to cut your lip and have to dash off to the emergency room to get stitches. The cut hurts. Stitches are painful. You don't have time to go to the emergency room. If you have insurance, your co-pay is expensive. If you don't have insurance, necessary medical treatment may be cost-prohibitive. You don't have time to miss work for those follow-up doctor's visits. To boot, you may have a scar that will stay with you for the rest of your life. *You throw the fucking glass away!* So why do you keep the cracked person? This doesn't make sense. I assure you, a tiny cut, a couple of stitches, and an afternoon in the ER pale in comparison to filing for divorce, sitting in a courtroom across the table from the person with whom you believed you would spend the rest of your life, and fighting over who gets to see the kids every other Tuesday and who gets to see them on Christmas Day in odd years. The assumption that we can fix our partner is a pattern which destines a relationship for certain failure. You can't and you won't fix anyone. It's not your job. It's each person's job to fix himself or herself—if he or she wants to.

In the chapter "If It's Broke, Don't Fix It," you will learn to identify whether your partner is broken and explore the difference between contributing to your partner's personal growth versus fixing. In the chapter "Two Wrongs Make a Fight," you will also learn the importance of fixing yourself before entering a relationship broken.

Fairy Tale

Life is not a fairy tale. You heard me. You are responsible for your own happiness. Life consists of ups and downs. There is *happy*. There is *no* happily ever after. We romanticize the "happily ever after." We *know* this isn't reality. For some reason, we crave escape. Unfortunately, by living in a fantasy world and setting unrealistic expectations for our lives, we will never be happy.

The first several months of a relationship may be the closest we get to the fairy tale. We cling desperately to this euphoric, albeit unsustainable, illusion of perfection, celebrating monthly anniversaries. When we begin to see our partner's flaws, when we catch a glimpse of our partner's quirks, when we get comfortable, when we argue or disagree, the vestiges of this reverie wilt away, leaving us longing for something we no longer have. In response, what do we do? We hold our breath for that storybook proposal, the one we can brag about to all our friends. We plan a wedding where, for one fleeting moment, we again momentarily occupy this illusory realm. We place so much emphasis on the wedding that it becomes more important than the thing it purports to celebrate. Sound familiar? Of course. These are patterns.

You will never be happy, and you will never choose the right partner if you do not make the crucial distinction between fantasy and reality. Life can be wonderful. You can be immensely happy. If, right now, you do not disabuse yourself of the notion that life will or should *always* be picture-perfect, or that your wedding is the most important day of your life, or that your partner should be some incarnation of Prince Charming or Cinderella, you will choose your partner for the *wrong* reasons and, in turn, you will choose the *wrong* partner.

You will spend your life chasing something unattainable. When you are more in love with the idea of being married than with the person to whom you are married, your marriage *will* fail. Throughout this book and, specifically, in the chapter "And They Lived Happily Never After," you will discover ways to avoid this pattern and enjoy a meaningful relationship without your unrealistic expectation of the happily ever after interfering with you attaining it.

Family

Love them or hate them, families are important for a slew of reasons. Family is instrumental in molding us. Our identities are tied to our families. The absence of family, such as in the case of the loss of or abandonment by a parent, shapes us just as much as, if not arguably more so than the presence of family. From our family, we learn how to love and be loved. A child who is abused by a parent may conflate abuse with love. In turn, in adulthood, this person may express love to his or her partner through abuse.

My mom often jokes, "If it wasn't for me, what would you have had to talk about in therapy?" I'll cut her some slack here. Even the most well-intentioned parents may unknowingly breed neuroses, dysfunctions, and insecurities in their children. Seemingly innocuous childhood experiences could lead to a gamut of behavioral or emotional conditions—such as codependency or abandonment issues. You get the picture. We are born a shapeless lump of clay, constantly evolving. By adulthood, we are mostly sculpted into the person we ultimately become. Although external experiences and traumas play a significant hand in shaping our personalities, our sensitivities, and our flaws, for most of us, our parents or parent figures are the ones sitting behind the potter's wheel, fastidiously kneading away.

Understanding your partner's family is sort of like that corner piece of the puzzle, the one that orients you. Your partner's family will provide invaluable clues into your partner's quirks, personality disorders, emotional conditions, or behavioral issues.

It isn't all doom and gloom, though. Your partner's family may reveal positive characteristics, such as empathy, warmth, inclusivity, and compassion. You want to know the bad and the ugly. You also want to know the good. Certain observations may clue you into the red flags. Others may support your decision to pursue the relationship.

Meeting your partner's family will not only provide you with information about your partner. It will also provide you with information about your partner's family. If your partner is close to his or her family, your partner's family will likely be involved in your lives. You should get to know them and determine whether you like them. You should also consider whether they like you. You are not just marrying your partner. You are marrying his or her family. When your partner's parents age, they may rely on you and your partner for assistance. At some point, they may even live with you. When your partner is close to his or her family, that family will be an integral part of your life. Likewise, if you are close to your family, your partner must get along with and willingly be close to your family as well.

In the chapter "Meet the Family," you will discover the reasons family is such an important part of your relationship. You will understand the ways a dysfunctional relationship between you and your partner's family could ultimately destroy your relationship.

Chapter 3:
What in the F-Word Is a Fundamental Value?

One of the most significant reasons people grow apart is that the glue needed to hold them together never existed in the first place. People mistake shared *interests* for shared *life values*. Dwelling so intensely on their superficial commonalities, they neglect to identify whether on a deeper and more meaningful level they *truly* have anything in common. They do not make the crucial inquiry into whether their perceived commonalities will carry them through more than the next several years or whether their shared interests are enough to sustain a successful co-parenting relationship.

Though it may seem unfathomable, what you *like* today will change tomorrow. Yet, fifty years from now, you will fundamentally *value* the same things you do today. In this way, interests are distinguishable from fundamental values. One's interests may evolve over the course of a lifetime. At different points in one's life, he or she may place greater priority on specific pursuits or hobbies. However, one's *fundamental* values at age twenty-five will typically be the same at age seventy-five.

To identify our fundamental values, we must first honestly define what we want in our lives, and the reason or reasons we want those things. Deciding what you want for the rest of your life may seem a daunting or even insurmountable undertaking when you can scarcely decide what you want to wear today and what you want to eat for dinner tonight. Let's think about this another way: during your festival-going phase, your bohemian-hippie phase, your vegan phase, what is it that has always remained important to you?

In identifying your fundamental values, you may find it helpful to examine what you value in this very moment of your life. Let's start by doing a little exercise that will help you to define your own fundamental values.

Exercise 1: What in the Heck Is Important to Me?

One of the best ways to start thinking about what you fundamentally value is to look at the things you value at this very moment of your life.

Below is a list of some values. Perhaps one or more resonates with you. Take a look at this list. Circle any values that resonate with you right now. To be clear, I am not asking you to actually define your fundamental values at this very juncture. I am simply asking you to identify what is important to you today, so that, later, you can distill from this list your *fundamental* values. If you value something that does not appear on this list, write it down. There is no wrong answer. Think of this as a getting-to-know-myself exercise:

- **Honesty**
- **Family Religion/Faith**
- **Politics**
- **Adventure**
- **Spirituality**
- **Education**
- **Tradition**
- **Career**
- **Health**
- **Loyalty**
- **Hobbies/Interests**
- **Wanderlust**
- **Independence**
- **Financial Stability**
- **Friendship**
- **Comfort**
- **Frugality**
- **Environmentalism**
- **Social activism**
- **Literariness**
- **Culinary pursuits**

From all the values you circled or wrote down, select the five that are most important to you *right now*, at this stage of your life. Make a list of the top five things you currently value, prioritizing them in order of importance. If two or three are equally important to you, don't worry. Write them all down below. Again, there are no wrong answers. Nobody will see your list. This is just for you, so don't be afraid to be completely honest.

1. _____

2. _____

3. _____

4. _____

5. _____

This exercise is intended to get you to start to think about what you value in life. Later, you will distinguish whether these values are fleeting or truly fundamental. You have to start somewhere. You must identify what is important to you, so you know where to begin your search for a life partner. We aimlessly select a partner without establishing the qualities that person should possess. This is akin to walking into a car dealership and telling the salesperson you want a "red car." By identifying the make and model of the car you like and the options you want on it, you will select the car that is right for you. In turn, you will enjoy a more fulfilling driving experience. Yes, you can still get a red one, but it should be the red one that gets good gas mileage and has working brakes. When it comes to relationships, so many of us settle for any red car convincing ourselves, "The brakes may not work all that well. I really like the color, though."

To understand what we fundamentally value, we must start by defining what we want for the rest of our lives and the reason it is important to us. Make no mistake. This is not easy. The me of today must decide what the me of the future wants—what forty-year-old *future* me wants and even what seventy-year-old *future* me wants. Usually, we are asked to do this before we have ever been married. We don't know what it feels like to be married or what it takes to sustain a marriage. We are faced with the conundrum of choosing a life partner based on what we *may* want thirty years from now, despite the fact that it's seemingly impossible to ascertain what we will want when we are in a very different place in our lives.

Your interests at age fifty may be different from your interests at age twenty. At your core, though, you are the same person you have always been. Your personality is established at a young age. Notwithstanding your mutable interests and personal evolution, what you fundamentally value will, for the most part, remain unchanged.

Our failure to ask these indispensable questions could, and likely will, result in precisely the outcome we seek to avoid. I hope you come away from this book having learned many invaluable lessons, among the most significant of which is: *your choice in a life partner will be the most important decision you ever make.* Allow me to repeat myself. The person with whom you choose to share your life is the most important decision you ever make. Why? The quality of the rest of your life largely hinges on the one with whom you choose to spend it. You will potentially spend the next sixty, seventy or even eighty years of your life with this person! So, choose wisely.

This person may be the mother or father to your children. This person will be the person with whom you make day-to-day decisions. This person will be the person who, if you are close to your family, will become a member of that family. This person will be there not only on your good days, but, more importantly, on those not-so-good days.

This person will (hopefully) be the one to care for you in the event you develop an illness. Perhaps you are undergoing a surgical procedure. You are under anesthesia and are not awake. The doctor runs out and asks your partner to make a split-second decision regarding your treatment. Will *this* person make the decision you would make on your own behalf? Do you feel confident that in the event of your untimely passing, this person will instill in your children the values you, yourself, would have instilled in them had you survived?

This all sounds very bleak. I do possess an uncanny flair for the dramatic. In all seriousness, though, you must contemplate such scenarios because the only thing certain about life is that it is completely uncertain. Such situations are real. Nobody is walking into a first or second date thinking about death. They're more worried about the shoes they chose to wear or how good their hair looks. Dare I say it? (I will dare). The questions are significantly more vital than your amazing outfit.

One way to identify your fundamental values is to understand the reason or reasons certain things are important to you. For instance, you may be in your twenties and love to travel. Eventually, you get married and have children. You are no longer able to travel as often as you once did, if at all. Certainly, even if you manage to travel frequently, you must consider children's bedtimes, visit age-appropriate attractions, and acknowledge your children's needs. Pounding endless tequila shots and dancing until six o'clock in the morning at a beachfront bar in Mykonos isn't in the cards anymore.

Despite what you may have thought, the need to travel may not be your *fundamental* value. Although this may sound like utter heresy at this very moment, there may be some deeper, underlying fundamental value, which temporarily manifests itself as a passion for travel. Your *fundamental* value is not travel itself, it's the rudimentary reason you are so passionate about travel. Travel fulfills some deeper, fundamental need. Travel might satiate your thirst for adventure. Travel is just one way this need for adventure is satisfied. When you have children, you may, at least for a time, be unable to travel, or to travel as frequently. Even when you do travel, you are far more encumbered than you were in your child-free days. However, even after having children, you are still seeking adventure, whether that means taking your children to the zoo, aquarium, or on hikes. You haven't stopped seeking adventure. You are merely seeking different adventures, appropriate to this particular stage of your life.

By identifying the underlying reason you are so passionate about travel, you discovered that your need for adventure permeates every facet of your existence. Your thirst for adventure, and not your need to travel, is your actual fundamental value. Consequently, you must find a partner who also fundamentally values adventure.

This type of self-evaluation allows you to pinpoint what is fundamentally important to you. In scrutinizing the reasons driving your passion for live music, or veganism, or social consciousness, you will start to reveal those deeper, enduring values.

Let's use our example of travel. If you have ascertained that your passion for travel is rooted in your need for adventure, then you must seek a partner who also fundamentally values adventure. One who enthusiastically approaches new experiences and opportunities is not well suited for someone who shies away from them. The adventurous partner will be continuously disappointed when the unadventurous partner avoids new experiences. The unadventurous partner will feel resentful when constantly forced outside of his or her comfort zone by the adventurous partner.

Identify your current passions and analyze whether they are sustainable into your thirties, forties, fifties, and sixties. If they are not, then they may not be *fundamental* values. Consider the underlying need that passion fulfills. Is this a need so vital to your existence that, without it, you would feel unfulfilled? If so, then the reason underlying the passion, as opposed to the specific passion itself, is likely your fundamental value.

With all of this in mind, let's do another exercise.

Exercise 2: What Do I Want in Life?

On the next page, you will find a chart, with columns respectively marked: 30s, 40s, 50s, 60s and 70s. In the column marked 30s, write down where you see yourself in your thirties. (If you are in your forties, then start with 40s. If you are in your fifties, then start with 50s, and so forth.) Be as specific as possible.

Do you see yourself owning a home? Describe where that home is. What city is it in? Do you have a favorite street you have always wanted to live on? Is it a single-story home or a two-story home? What style is it? Traditional? Modern? How much did that home cost? How old are you when you buy this home? What do you do for a living that enables you to buy this home? How long did you save up to buy this home? Remember, you are defining for yourself what you want. This is your life. You get to narrate the story. I urge you to be realistic. This exercise is designed to help you ascertain what you fundamentally value and, in turn, recognize which qualities *you* are looking for in a life-partner. At the same time, do not sell yourself short. You believe you will own a five-million-dollar mansion by the time you are thirty-seven. Whether or not you actually own this mansion by the time you are thirty-seven, you should seek a partner who is so ambitious and driven that he or she is inclined to work alongside you to achieve this lofty goal.

If you find this exercise difficult, that's okay. It is. Spend some time on it. The journey is deeply personal, and it is yours—not mine, not anyone else's.

30s	40s	50s

60s	70s

Once you have completed this exercise, step back and look at what you have written. Is there a theme that runs throughout? Would you like to own property or are you content renting? Do you want children or not? Are children a maybe? Do you see your children attending private school or public school? How many hours a week do you work? Would you prefer your spouse to stay home and care for your children while you work to support the family? Are you comfortable being the sole provider for your family—like really and truly? Do you like going out all the time or are you a homebody? Do you work to live or live to work? Do you need to travel? When you travel, are you satisfied traveling within your own state or country, or do you have an insatiable need to explore foreign countries? What in your life makes you feel fulfilled? What makes you feel unfulfilled? What are your passions and hobbies? Are those passions specific to your life right now, or do you think these are passions and hobbies you will have for the rest of your life as you grow older and your priorities change? Have you always had these passions and hobbies? If not, what passions and hobbies have you had for most, if not your entire life? Do you prefer to live in a big city or a small town? Are you adamant about residing in the same city as your family or would you be content living elsewhere? Is religion important to you? What are your political beliefs? Are you a dog or a cat person? Even if you are an animal lover, do you want the actual responsibility of owning a pet? Do you value higher education or is a high school degree sufficient? Are you a strict vegan or vegetarian who could never be with someone who ate meat? Are you a meat eater who could never be with someone who was a vegetarian or vegan?

The list goes on and on. I could easily devote ten pages to questions like these. I won't bore and overwhelm you. I offer these questions to get you to think about the type of questions you should be asking yourself—questions that will lead you to the answers you must find.

This is a good place for me to pause and share with you a personal experience:

When I was seventeen, I met my, now, ex-husband. We didn't get married until I was twenty-six. We got divorced when I was twenty-seven. Congratulations, you did the math correctly. We were married for just over a year.

He was kind, fun and had a good heart. I was attending one of the top private high schools in Los Angeles. I was a straight-A student, the president of three clubs, an accomplished pianist, a yoga instructor, and an all-around overachiever. (Think Lisa Simpson, only a little edgier.) When we met, he was in college. Although incredibly intelligent, he was failing the majority of his classes. Education and academic success were not at all the priorities to him that they were to me. He went to college upon the insistence of his parents. He had no interest in higher education. In stark contrast, I was applying to some of the most competitive colleges in the country and planned to, thereafter, attain a secondary degree. He pursued me. His warmth and kindness won me over. At seventeen, I was oblivious that our seemingly superficial differences were so fundamental that they ultimately drove us apart. (Ironically, our superficial similarities attracted us to each other, but were insufficient to sustain an enduring relationship.)

By the time he graduated college, he had brought his grades up from Ds and Fs to As and Bs. He went on to obtain an MBA. To this day, I don't know if he did this because he genuinely wanted to, or because at that point, knowing I had gotten accepted to law school, he felt he had to do so.

I believed we had so much in common. So did he. We both loved punk music and going to shows. We both had a fascination with Japanese culture. It was impossible to look at us and think we were anything short of soulmates. Sadly, our mutual interests did not translate into shared fundamental values. We were so young and naive, neither one of us understood this at the time.

The demise of our relationship came when I took the Bar Exam. Naturally, he was the first person I called after I completed the grueling three-day test. He had watched me devote the preceding several months of my life virtually exclusively to studying. He knew how hard I had worked. Nevertheless, he was totally indifferent. I didn't quite understand it at the time. I was hurt by his response. Our wedding was four months away and I felt that the person to whom I was about to commit the rest of my life should have been excited that I completed one of the most formidable challenges of my existence.

Of course, despite my reservations, I did marry him. After all, we had already paid the deposits to the venue and wedding band, sent out the save the dates and my dress had been purchased and fitted. No sir, there was no turning back now. The proverbial train had left the station and I was unwilling to make the decision I intuitively knew I should.

I went on to practice law. Things got worse. I recall one specific incident where he sat down on the couch, angrily deleting songs from his iPod. (Yes, this was back when dinosaurs roamed the Earth.) When I asked him what he was doing, he responded, "I don't like these songs!" The songs to which he was referring were songs I thought we *both* loved—or so he had maintained for the previous ten years.

I will spare you the banal details. We decided to end our marriage. I felt he had become complacent. He felt resentful—an emotion, as you will learn, that almost always connotes and accompanies the demise of a relationship. For the past ten years, the boy I met at the Coffee Bean and Tea Leaf, who was failing out of college, felt that in order to get the girl and keep the girl, he had to become something he was not.

We were both oblivious to the fact that he had exhaustingly devoted the previous ten years of our relationship to trying to "keep up" with me, until he finally recognized he could not and no longer wanted to. I do not blame him. I would never have wanted that for him. He was not deliberately deceiving me. He genuinely believed he loved to travel and go out on the weekends—things that were fundamentally important to me. He had convinced himself the only way to be with me was to embrace *my* values. Nobody can sustain a charade for a prolonged period of time. Nobody should have to.

He was not wrong. I was not right. We were just different. Our upbringings, our goals, our backgrounds, our fundamental values were so disparate that, instead of growing together, we grew apart. He is a wonderful human being who deserved to be with somebody who shared his values and not someone with whose values he needed to compete or keep up.

I share this example with you not for my own catharsis—five years of therapy, several relationships and another very happy marriage later, trust me, I'm fine. I share this with you to point out that defining core values, and distinguishing them from superficial values, is imperative. And this brings me back to my point. . . .

Look at your answers to Exercise 2. I asked you to define where you see yourself in each decade of your life. I tasked you with defining what you want. No matter how different each decade may look, there is a common thread or threads that run through each decade of your life. While you will unequivocally find yourself in different places during the various stages of your life, there are several themes that are unchanging. Yes, I love music, but my taste in music is ever evolving. I used to go to at least one to two shows a week. Now, I'm lucky if I make it to two a year. I still love music. I'm just tired. Shows are no longer vital to my existence. Twenty-three-year-old me would have vehemently disagreed. The love of music that my ex-husband and I shared was not a fundamental value. It was not enough to hold us together. (No joke, a month into dating my current husband, I tried to end our relationship because he didn't know I was quoting *The Big Lebowski*. He had never seen the film. Don't worry. I love him anyway. Thankfully, at this point, when I say, "That rug really tied the room together," he gets it. Crisis averted.)

What are fundamental values? Fundamental values are the things that have always been important to you and that you know will always remain important to you, no matter what stage of your life you may be in. For example, I am extremely close to my family. It is vital to me that my partner loves my family and wants to spend time with them. It is crucial to me that my family loves and accepts my partner. It is equally important to me that my partner is close to his family and values family as much as I do. I don't feel he could possibly understand how very essential my relationship to my family is unless he, himself, values his own. We will discuss this value in greater detail a little later on. I point it out now to distinguish between something as superficial as my love of live music from something as elementary as the importance of family. Two people can be successful life partners when one loves Beyoncé and the other can't stand her. (Here's the part where Beyoncé fans lose their minds.) But two people cannot be successful life partners when one values family and the other is indifferent, or even annoyed by it.

Other fundamental values include financial stability and goal achievement. I have represented women and men whose marriages fell apart because their spouses were total workaholics. The workaholic spouse seemingly valued a career over his or her spouse, children, and other personal obligations. Work, *per se*, is not the fundamental value, though. The devotion to work hints at something deeper. The workaholic may fundamentally value the financial security that accompanies hard work. Or perhaps the workaholic spouse seeks and derives validation from his or her accomplishments. The underlying fundamental value is specific to the individual. The devotion to this individual's job clues us into what he or she fundamentally values.

Regardless of the workaholic's impetus for prioritizing his or her career, the workaholic is poorly suited for someone who could care less about work. The workaholic is attracted to his or her opposite, initially fetishizing the notion of apathy toward one's work. The workaholic is almost turned on by the fact that his or her partner can so easily reject something that otherwise controls the workaholic. A part of him wishes that he too could be blasé about work. Through his or her partner, the workaholic vicariously fantasizes about a life free from the clutches of a job.

Yet, once the initial mystique fades, the workaholic is reminded of the reasons he or she fundamentally values work. The workaholic will perceive his or her partner as irresponsible and lose interest. In turn, the workaholic's partner will feel judged, subordinate, and grow resentful. The workaholic will bury himself or herself deeper into work, in part as a means of avoiding the struggles in the relationship, and in other part to derive personal validation from his or her job. The work is an old friend that provides the workaholic with familiar comfort. The workaholic's partner will feel neglected and either grow depressed, have an affair, or both.

Another important fundamental value is education. Before you get huffy, I do not purport that two people with different educational backgrounds cannot have a successful relationship. I am using education as another illustration of a fundamental value. One who graduates from high school and chooses not to pursue a college education champions different things than one who graduates from college and decides to go pursue a doctorate. This may be an indication of disparate life goals, and, accordingly, different fundamental values. One who values education may fundamentally value the accumulation of knowledge. Alternatively, he or she may fundamentally value the financial stability that could accompany higher education. Again, you must take the time to understand the underlying fundamental value that the attainment of education satisfies. As an aside—a value is not good or bad. A value is personal. You must define your values for yourself, so you can look for a life partner who shares the same core values. Put another way, the right partner is one who is on the *same level* as you.

For example, many of my male clients married (and went on to divorce) younger, highly attractive women. In each such case, my male client—the husband—has at least a college degree, if not an MBA or JD. (For some reason, they always have an MBA or a JD.) His wife has a high school diploma. The husband is usually in his late thirties. When he marries his wife, she is in her early twenties. The wife is fun and good-looking. At times, she can be "ditzy." This is one of the traits the husband finds to be "endearing" and "cute." After the couple has children and the husband's career grows increasingly demanding, the trait he once characterized as "endearing" and "cute," he now finds annoying. Even though the wife has not changed, the husband starts to crave more intelligent conversation. He wants a partner who is intellectually on his level. The marriage falls apart. In no way do I purport to pass judgment. Countless highly intelligent and successful individuals—Mark Zuckerberg, Steve Jobs, and Bill Gates, to name a few—never graduated from college. I share this example because it is so prevalent. It perfectly illustrates the way marriages fall apart when two people place greater emphasis on superficial qualities than on shared fundamental values.

Let's look at another example. Samantha pursues a medical degree. By the time she completes her fellowship, she would have been in school for fourteen years. She does this because she established that she loves to help people. She also values financial security. Let's say she chooses a life partner, Jake, who did not go to college. Jake is satisfied renting an apartment. He values financial security. However, financial security to him does not equate to a multimillion-dollar home or lavish vacations. Samantha and Jake have similar interests and enjoy their time together. With his high school degree, Jake finds a job at which he earns a modest, albeit comfortable, living. He has no aspirations of working his way up the corporate ladder. He is content in his position. It pays the bills. He lives paycheck-to-paycheck. Samantha amasses sizable savings.

No matter how much Samantha and Jake both may love the show *Seinfeld* or share a passion for yoga, they want different things in their lives. In the beginning, they will bond over the fact that they both love Christy's heated vinyasa class or that their favorite episode of *Seinfeld* is the one where George gifts a discounted cashmere sweater to Elaine, hoping she doesn't notice the red mark on it. (I know I'm really dating myself here. But *Seinfeld* will forever be a classic.) Samantha and Jake are extremely physically attracted to one another.

Several years go by. Samantha—who is, by this point, a successful cardiologist—wants to purchase a multimillion-dollar home that she can afford only if Jake earns an income commensurate to hers. He does not. Samantha grows resentful that Jake's income is insufficient for the couple to achieve her goal. Jake feels inadequate and has an affair with a woman who does not make him feel deficient—a woman who is on Jake's level and is content with the modest lifestyle with which Jake is happy. Although Samantha always knew of Jake's aspirations and he of hers, Samantha now unfairly wishes Jake strove for more. No, not even Christy's hot yoga class can save them now.

Happiness does not mean a multimillion-dollar home. Someone who feels owning a multimillion-dollar home is important should find a partner who feels owning a multimillion-dollar home is equally important. *Sharing fundamental values means that, when you expect certain things in life, you should find a partner who also expects those same things.*

So, now that you know the reason shared fundamental values are so critical to the success of a relationship, how do you determine what you fundamentally value?

Exercise 3: What Do I *Fundamentally* Value?

Review your answers in Exercise 1. Then, look at all of your answers in Exercise 2. Are there any common themes you can detect?

For instance, you may love nothing more than going to concerts. While you may see yourself attending concerts in your forties and even fifties, perhaps you won't attend with the same frequency you do when you are in your twenties and thirties. Going to concerts is not really a fundamental value so much as it is a fleeting interest. What is it that underlies your love of concert-going? Is it a passion for the arts? Is it the need for new and exciting experiences, or possibly adventure? Is it the social aspect? The deeper fundamental value most likely manifests itself as a passion for attending concerts. The concert-going, itself, is not actually the fundamental value. Or maybe it is. Perhaps concert-going is so fundamentally important to you that you work just to pay for tickets and intend to do so forever.

By examining the things that are important to you *right now*, you determine whether they will be important to you in the future. If these things are unlikely to be fundamentally important to you in the future, then take a step back and ask yourself what deeper need or desire these things fulfill. Those deeper, underlying needs are likely the fundamental values.

Let's look at another example. Right now, you may really value alone time. You may absolutely love hanging out with your friends and family. You also derive so much joy from spending a night by yourself, watching whatever you want on your favorite streaming platform. Or maybe you love going to dinner or a bar on your own. You want to be in a relationship, but you deem it important to have some alone time—so much so, in fact, that you listed it as one of your values in Exercise 1.

Now, in response to where you see yourself in your thirties, you wrote: "I own a house. That house has an extra bedroom. In it is my office. I have my own space where I can go to escape. My wife is cool when, some nights, I go in there to play Fortnite, or whatever the equivalent to Fortnite will be in the year 2035."

In response to where you see yourself in your forties, you wrote: "I have a wife and two children. Every year, my wife takes a weekend trip with her friends. I take a weekend trip with my friends."

In response to where you see yourself in your fifties, you wrote: "I'd love to retire early, sit on my porch all day and read books."

Most likely, you are not the type who will suddenly turn forty-three and decide you want a needy partner, who must spend every waking minute with you. You fundamentally value independence. You meet a partner who also happens to love Fortnite. A match made in heaven though it may seem, your mutual love of Fortnite may not render this partner right for you. This person may always want to play Fortnite with you and does not understand your need for alone time. Your task is to ascertain whether your partner is codependent, not whether he or she is obsessed with Fortnite.

Take a look at what you wrote in Exercises 1 and 2. Is there something you value right now that carries into your thirties, forties, and fifties? Can you spot a theme?

On the next page, write down three to five underlying fundamental values that seem to run through each decade:

1. _____

2. _____

3. _____

4. _____

5. _____

Are you coming up short? Look back at the decisions you've made in your life to date. Is family important to you? Is education important to you? Is bringing up your children in a specific faith or in a particular way important to you?

Turning to our cardiologist, Samantha; in her teen years, she applied to and went to college. In her early twenties, she decided she wanted a career that afforded her financial stability. She decided to apply to medical school. In her thirties, after several years as a successful cardiologist, she decided she wanted to purchase a large and expensive home. Samantha's value is not education, alone. She values a certain lifestyle she expects her education to afford her. She is not an academic, *per se*. Her value is not strictly knowledge, but the financial security that will most likely accompany her choices.

Let's look at another example. In his twenties, Adam wants to be a writer. Adam doesn't care if he must wait tables to pay rent. He doesn't care if he must live paycheck-to-paycheck. More than anything, he wants to lead a life pursuing his passion. Adam will be content living in a studio apartment into his thirties, or even into his fifties, so long as he is writing. Adam has a sister who is two years younger. He and his sister are best friends. When his sister moved from New York to Los Angeles, he also moved from New York to Los Angeles. He could not bear to be three thousand miles away from her. What values are fundamental to Adam?

This isn't a trick question. Obviously, Adam values family. He also values his passion—writing—over material possession or even financial stability. Adam and our cardiologist would be oh so very wrong for one another. As obvious as this may appear to you, dear reader, I have seen many-an-Adam and our cardiologist walk into my office. During their courtship, they had "so much fun together." They just neglected to consider the next ten, twenty or fifty years of their lives.

Sometimes, viewing your own relationship with objectivity is difficult. It requires you to step outside of yourself, to observe your life from a distance. Study my examples. Think of some of your past relationships. Now that you are no longer in the relationship, you are in the position to objectively analyze whether you and your ex-partner shared fundamental values. What were your ex-partner's values? How did they differ from yours? Why did the relationship end? Think of someone you know who you consider to be in a successful relationship. What values do the people in this successful relationship have? Why do you consider their relationship to be successful?

If we cannot define what we want in our lives, and distill from this our fundamental values, then we are left to rely on attraction and chance—each of which may seem enough temporarily, but neither of which translates into a successful, lifelong partnership.

By failing to identify whether you and your partner share fundamental values early in the relationship, you will become emotionally invested in someone with whom you are likely incompatible. The more entrenched in the relationship you become, the less likely you are to objectively scrutinize it. Of course, to do so would mean the potentially ominous end of the relationship.

If you cannot define for yourself what you want in life, then how do you expect to find a partner who fits into the life you want?

The qualities that first draw us to our partner—a shared interest or hobby, or physical attraction—are not necessarily the qualities that make for a successful long-lasting relationship. You and your partner decide to get married. You do love each other. Sadly, love is not always enough to sustain a relationship over the course of a lifetime. I'm sorry, John Lennon. Love is *not* all you need. People do not realize this when they get married. They come to learn it as they attempt to navigate life with a partner whose values are not aligned with their own. Ultimately, rather than accomplish anything, they end up butting heads. Neither way is right or better. Had each of them taken the time to identify the other's fundamental values when they first met (rather than mistaking their mutual passion for spin class and dogs for shared values), perhaps they would not have ended up another cliché.

While the other F-Words are addressed in no particular order, "fundamental values" is deliberately addressed *first*. The reason for this is simple. When you and your partner do not share fundamental values, the relationship cannot and will not succeed. Nothing else matters. Love alone is insufficient to sustain a long-lasting and mean-ingful relationship without the necessary glue to hold two people together through their lifetimes. A successful relationship is pred-icated on so much more. Before you make the very serious deci-sion to commit your life to someone, you must determine whether you share fundamental values. Later on we will explore the F-Word foundation in greater detail, but for the time being, you need only know that without fundamental values there can be no founda-tion. This would be like placing a block of concrete onto a pile of sand and trying to build a house. The sand will move, the block of concrete will slip and the structure that rests on top of the concrete block will topple.

The absence of shared fundamental values should serve as a flagrant indicator for you to move on. No matter how infatuated you may be, you do not matriculate to building a foundation with a person with whom you do not share fundamental values. Period.

Chapter 4:
I'm Sorry, But You Don't Get the Job

"Judge a man by his questions rather than his answers." —Voltaire

So, how do you determine whether you and your partner share fundamental values *prior* to beginning the relationship?

Once you become emotionally invested, you will find it far more difficult to extricate yourself from the relationship, even when you know you should. Before you allow yourself to get emotionally involved, you must determine whether the relationship is even worth pursuing. This is accomplished by treating each date as a job interview. I am not suggesting that dates be devoid of flirtation. Go ahead, cake on that makeup. Show a little leg. Sexual compatibility is an essential part of a relationship. I am also of the belief that true compatibility engenders physical attraction.

"He's so cute." "She's so hot." These do not translate to long-term compatibility. In many countries, marriages are arranged. The partners do not meet until their wedding day. Attraction grows between two people as they grow together. Through teamwork and communication, they come to trust and respect each other and, in turn, feel comfortable being vulnerable and intimate with one another. Is this true in 100 percent of arranged marriages? Of course not. There simultaneously exists a tragic culture of forced marriages in which the rates of domestic violence are high. I use this example not to glorify arranged marriages, but to illustrate that arranged marriages often succeed because the bride's and groom's parents share similar fundamental values. Consequently, the bride and groom automatically share fundamental values. The families know their children will be compatible, as the families themselves have instilled similar beliefs and values in their children.

Today, so many dates are the inevitable result of a mutual swipe right. Online dating inundates us with options. It can be overwhelming and simultaneously discouraging. Rather than predicating our decision to go on a date with someone based on chemistry or flirtation, we base it on whether we finally stumble across a picture that piques our interest after swiping left for five to ten minutes. The nature of modern dating is such that we approach partner selection from a superficial standpoint, as opposed to selecting a partner with whom we might share fundamental values. I most certainly do not knock online dating. I know many happily married people who met their partners on various dating platforms. I do believe that online dating makes it more difficult to glean key information, which would otherwise be more readily available through an organic meeting. This does not mean you should abandon online dating. It does mean the job interview is all the more critical.

Okay, it's your first date. You've picked the perfect outfit. You shaved, primped, and groomed. You even washed your car for the first time in three years. Have you contemplated what is arguably more important—the questions you will ask? I hate to break it to you (let's face it, that's the reason I'm here), your date's favorite color is the least important piece of information you need to know. And, yes, she may be impressed by that Drakkar Noir you scrupulously spritzed behind your right ear. That fact, alone, does not anoint her marriage material. Truly shocking, I know.

You have devoted a fair amount of time identifying your fundamental values and exploring the reasons it is so important that you and your partner share them. The questions you ask should be geared toward establishing whether you and your date share the *same* fundamental values and goals in life. Since you know your fundamental values, you are in the position to come up with very pointed questions to elicit the responses you are seeking from your date.

Does a first date even lead to a second? Remember, so many relationships fail because two people do not share fundamental values. Do the work *now* to prevent a relationsh*t-show later.

Let me give you an example. Suppose you have identified one of your fundamental values to be family. You have a sibling. Spending quality time with your family is important. Even though some days, you question whether you may have been adopted by those weirdos, you are incredibly close to your parents. Living relatively close to your family is crucial. In fact, your parents have been happily married for over forty years and, their quirks aside, you consider theirs to be a model of a successful relationship. Your family has dinner together at least once a week. They do fun activities together. Your family is so cool, most of your friends wish they were a member.

Now, let's say your partner comes from a broken home. His parents divorced when he was younger. He was never that close to his mother. In fact, he couldn't relate to her. Your partner is fairly close to his father, but nowhere near as close to his as you are to yours. His mother lives in Miami. You and your partner live together in San Francisco. Your partner sees his father about twice a year and talks to him on the phone about once a week, oftentimes, out of obligation. Your partner has a sister. They are not particularly close. In fact, he doesn't really care for his sister and never spends any time with her except at family functions. Your partner begrudgingly spends time with your family. Spending time with your family is an uncomfortable reminder to him of the problems he has with his own. He is unable to separate the way he feels about his own family from the general notion of family. Nevertheless, he knows family is important to you, so he shows up to Thanksgiving dinner and your cousin's wedding. Sometimes, he makes excuses as to the reason he cannot attend a birthday dinner or a Sunday game night.

Several years go by and you decide to get married. A year later, you have a child. Your partner demands to move to Austin, Texas, threatening to take your child with him. He says, "Join me or don't." "Why Austin?" you ask. Your partner claims, "I don't know how we can afford to continue to live in San Francisco." Sure, San Francisco is expensive. However, you and your partner have decent jobs and you have been living comfortably in San Francisco. You know the cost of living has been lower in Austin than San Francisco for many years. But you want to be close to your family, particularly now that you have a child. Your partner does not understand this. He is perfectly content with living far away from his family and has been doing so. This causes problems in the marriage, which ultimately lead to divorce.

Following the divorce, your partner moves to Austin. You are faced with the choice of also moving to Austin or remaining in San Francisco and sharing custody of your child from a distance. I have represented a number of clients whose ex-partner lives in another state. The children are shuttled back and forth, forced to travel by plane for court-ordered visits. The children are often accompanied by a flight attendant, who is a total stranger to them. The situation is far from ideal.

I know these are not the types of scenarios you envision when you are in your twenties or thirties and dating someone who also loves hiking and avocado toast as much as you do. They are the types of things you *should* be thinking about, though. Ending this relationship now is significantly easier than putting your five-year-old son on a plane and saying goodbye to him for four weeks at a time every summer.

The questions you ask now, or the questions you *fail* to ask, will have such far-reaching impact that they could detrimentally affect your future children—should you decide to have them. Sure, when that girl you met on Tinder looks so sexy in those yoga pants, you aren't thinking about your future children, right?

So, what questions do we ask? How do we ask them without coming off as a complete psycho who is eager to get married after the first date? Let's go back to our example. Family is important to you. You may wish to ask: "Do you have any siblings?" "Older or younger?" "Where does your family live?" If they live in another state or country, you might ask: "Do you see them often?" "Do you talk often?" On a first date, you need not ask such personal questions as: "Are your parents still together?" or "Are you close to your parents?" These are questions that may be reserved for a later date . . . if there is a later date.

The answers to these safe questions will provide you with some clues. If you live in Los Angeles and the answer to: "Where do your parents live?" is "Idaho," observe your date's face as he or she answers. Does your date say "Idaho" and sadly look down at the floor? This could suggest your date is estranged from his or her family. It could also mean your date is sad that his or her family lives in a different state. These may not be questions to pursue further on a first or even second date. You should make a mental note to yourself to learn more on a future date—provided there is a future date. Does your date nonchalantly answer "Idaho" and move on to the next question? Observe your date's demeanor as he or she answers your questions. In our example, when your date talks about his or her family, does he or she seem happy? Listen to the cadence of your date's voice. Does he or she seem excited? What is the inflection of your date's voice when he or she answers? Does your date get quieter or louder? Does he or she try to change the subject? Does your date come right out and say, "I don't speak to my father. He's an asshole."

Such observations will not be limited to the subject of family, alone. You will ask specific questions to determine whether your date shares *your* fundamental values. As your date answers your questions, evaluate his or her body language, inflection, and answers.

You are familiar with the gamut of human emotions. You, yourself, experience them. You know that when you are sad, your voice gets lower and more monotone. Your shoulders may slouch forward, or you may bow your head. You know when you are excited, your voice grows louder and possibly more high-pitched. You know that when you feel uncomfortable, you avoid eye contact. When you are confident, you gaze directly into the eyes of the person to whom you are speaking. The way you emote is largely similar to the way others emote. You know what happens to your voice and your body language when you are upset, so you can discern from another's body language when he or she is upset. Rather, we must listen to and truly hear the answers we receive, even if they are not the answers we were hoping for.

In our example, the mere fact that one lives far from his or her parents is not, in and of itself, dispositive of anything. It is just one piece of the puzzle. Your mission is to put the pieces together to understand the bigger picture. That may require several dates, or you may know after the first date.

I once went on a second date with someone who made fun of a gentleman at the bar we were at. This gentleman, let's call him Dan, appeared to have a visible drug and alcohol problem. Dan, who I actually knew, had a good heart. He seemed sad and deeply troubled, turning to drugs and alcohol to cope. I don't know whether my date was nervous and trying to relate to me or whether he genuinely lacked empathy. I suspect it was the latter. To me, he lacked the fundamental value of compassion. It took two dates for me to ascertain this. I liked him enough after the first date to go on a second. He made it to the second round of the interview process. Ultimately, he did not get the job.

Here's another example. Education is one of your fundamental values. You want to know whether your date is tenacious and goal oriented. You are. You want to be with someone who is not afraid of hard work and is willing to do whatever is necessary to attain his or her goals. That is the way you are too. On your first date, you may wish to ask: "Where did you go to school?" "What did you major in?" Yes, this is cliché first date "small talk." A first date is not the time to talk about how you have trust issues on account of that one time, when you were six, your mom forgot to pick you up from school and you had to wait in the principal's office until seven o'clock at night.

Asking the right questions is only one part of the job interview. The second part is listening to the answers you are given. Maya Angelou said: "When someone shows you who they are, believe them the first time." You want to know the truth. Listen. Pay attention. So many people hear the answers they want, rather than the answers they are given. In an all-too-common example, a man will enter a relationship with a woman nearing her forties. This woman makes it clear she wants children. The man may want children too, but he is in no rush. The man is not completely oblivious. He is well aware that a woman's fertility is finite. He knows this woman is approaching the age at which conception will become more difficult, if not impossible. He enjoys this woman's company and avoids broaching the subject, hoping her biology will somehow change. Meanwhile, this woman nervously waits for the right opportunity to revisit the conversation. She doesn't want to waste what little time she has with someone who isn't ready to have children with her in the near future. Ultimately, the man is faced with two choices: 1) break up with this woman because he isn't ready to be a father, or 2) stay with someone he may not be ready to commit to, and father a child before he's prepared to do so. Now, he's emotionally invested. He didn't listen when an almost forty-year-old woman told him she wanted children.

It is far easier to turn down a second date with a person you barely know than to break up with someone you've loved for two years, or even two months into a relationship. Asking questions allows us to determine whether a second date is even appropriate. By doing so, we save ourselves and our date from potential hurt.

You know your fundamental values. Now it's time to figure out which questions to ask, to determine whether your date's fundamental values align with yours.

Exercise 4: Preparing for the Job Interview

You were raised Catholic. You fundamentally value religion and spirituality. You want children and you want to raise your children Catholic. You go to church on Sundays and want a partner who will attend church with you. During your first or second date, you should definitely mention your Catholic upbringing. Let your date know that you go to church on Sundays. Gauge his or her reaction. Find a good point in the conversation to casually weave in the fact that you attended Catholic school as a child. Maybe your date will say something like, "I know all about guilt. I have a Jewish mother," to which you may respond with something like, "Haha. Yeah. Well, I went to Catholic school, so I'm no stranger to guilt." Then, you will segue into the topic by cracking a joke and saying something like, "I must be a glutton for punishment because I still go to church every Sunday morning." That will lead you into your line of questions: "So, Jewish mother, eh? Are you religious?" "How do you feel about religion in general?" "How do you feel about the fact that I go to church?"

When you are so hung up on trying to impress your date that you suppress a critical fact, you are doing both yourself and your date a great disservice. It doesn't matter that you are really into this person. If this person possesses a negative view of or is simply apathetic to religion, then this isn't the right person for you. Don't waste your date's time as well as your own. It is far better to identify your differences than invest in and pursue a relationship that will ultimately fail.

Inevitably, you will be somewhat nervous on your first date. You may not recall the exact questions you want or need to ask. You should generate a list of questions to ask so that you don't have to think of them on the spot.

For each of your fundamental values, make a list of three possible questions you could ask your date to determine whether he or she shares the same fundamental values. You do not need to memorize these. If you don't get around to asking them, that's perfectly okay. This exercise is designed to get you to start thinking about the types of questions you should ask.

Remember, dating is a job interview. When you walk into a job interview, the interviewer has a list of questions prepared for you. When you steer the conversation in a different direction, the interviewer may deviate from the questions. Ultimately, the interviewer will still elicit the information he or she needs to ascertain whether you qualify for the position. The interviewer listens to your answers and takes them at face value. A company would not hire you if you were not right for the job. You should not date someone if he or she is not right for your life. Would an employer hire you just because you are handsome? No. Would a college accept you because your only qualification is that you are nice? No. So why would you commit to someone merely because he or she is nice or attractive? The answer is that you shouldn't. It's not enough. Sure, when you are casually dating someone with no intention of getting married, none of this really matters. Then again, you are reading this book because you want to find a life partner. Ask questions. Ask the *right* questions. Accept the answers you receive. This is, quite literally, the most important decision you will ever make in your life.

FUNDAMENTAL VALUE 1:

Write down your fundamental value:

_____

_____

List 3 questions you could ask that would provide some insight into whether your date shares this fundamental value:

1. _____
_____?

2. _____
_____?

3. _____
_____?

FUNDAMENTAL VALUE 2:

Write down your fundamental value:

_____

_____

List 3 questions you could ask that would provide some insight into whether your date shares this fundamental value:

1. _____
_____?

2. _____
_____?

3. _____
_____?

FUNDAMENTAL VALUE 3:

Write down your fundamental value:

_____

_____

List 3 questions you could ask that would provide some insight into whether your date shares this fundamental value:

  1. _____

     _____?

  2. _____

     _____?

  3. _____

     _____?

FUNDAMENTAL VALUE 4:

Write down your fundamental value:

_____

_____

List 3 questions you could ask that would provide some insight into whether your date shares this fundamental value:

  1. _____

     _____?

  2. _____

     _____?

  3. _____

     _____?

FUNDAMENTAL VALUE 5:

Write down your fundamental value:

_____

_____

List 3 questions you could ask that would provide some insight into whether your date shares this fundamental value:

1. _____

_____?

2. _____

_____?

3. _____

_____

To be clear, your date should not consist of an exhaustive list of questions. I merely suggest that you pepper a few pointed questions into the conversation that will provide you with some idea as to whether your date shares at least some of your fundamental values. By properly conducting the job interview, you can easily elicit answers to questions that will determine whether another date is warranted.

If your date answers your questions correctly on the first date, he or she advances to the second date. The interview doesn't end on the first date. It continues through the second date and every encounter thereafter until you decide if this is the person with whom you wish to share your life. The questions are contrived for precisely that purpose. Summon your inner Barbara Walters and conduct that hard-hitting interrogation, uncovering every sordid detail.

Chapter 5:
How Many Light Bulbs Does a Narcissist Need? None.
He Uses Gaslighting.

"Narcissism is not about self-love. It's a clinical trait that belies a deep sense of emptiness, low self-esteem, emotional detachment, self-loathing, extreme problems with intimacy." —Drew Pinsky

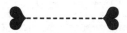

L et's talk about a fun subject—narcissists. More specifically, are you dating one? Indeed, this seems oddly specific. Such inquiry, at least from my perspective, is a critical part of the job interview—so much so, in fact, that it is deserving of its own chapter. Determining whether your potential life partner is a narcissist or possesses narcissistic tendencies is important—like really, really fucking important! The ugliest, longest, and by far, most soul-crushing divorces I have ever witnessed involved a narcissist on the opposing side.

Let's start with the requisite disclaimer: this book is not about narcissists. I am not a mental health professional. I cannot diagnose anyone with a personality disorder.

I *do* possess the keen ability to sniff out a narcissist. Call it a "talent," honed over so many years of working with them. Notwithstanding the varying degrees of manipulation, gaslighting, and subversion, all narcissists behave the very *same* way in divorce litigation—proving it all too easy to spot one.

As much as narcissists would love the fact that I devote an entire chapter to them, I don't do it to flatter them. No, there's a special place in Hell reserved for narcissists as punishment for the sadistic torture they deliberately inflict upon my clients and their children. I do it because—as much as you want to avoid divorce altogether— you most definitely want to avoid divorcing a narcissist. This means never forming a relationship with one in the first place. Trust me. You will leave your divorce emotionally, psychologically, and financially crushed, and you may end up alienated from your child or children. I know this sounds sensationalistic. You might think, "There she goes with the hyperbolizing again." I assure you. I am dead serious. I recall this meme. Pictured in it was a skeleton with its head folded into its hands. The caption read: "Don't mind me. I'm waiting for a narcissist to apologize." It would be funny if it was not so brutally true. I have seen things—horrific things. I do not want to see *you* on the receiving end of what a narcissist will inevitably put you through in a divorce.

There is an explanation for this. Narcissists want to win. They want to be in control. They don't want to be perceived as anything less than perfect. I often watch couples play out the control issues in their relationship through the divorce process. For example, a wife who might have felt controlled by her husband during their marriage may attempt to usurp this power and control by seeking sole physical custody of their children or securing a sizable support order. A controlling husband may cut off his wife's access to any joint accounts, leaving her penniless for several months until she is able to get a court hearing and procure a support order. A woman who was hurt by her husband's affair may retaliate by getting a restraining order against him or absconding with their children. It's Shakespearean, really. Retaliation, punishment, revenge—these motives are the driving force behind so much divorce litigation. Thus, it comes as no surprise that a narcissist—who must remain in control and feels self-important—will be fundamentally challenged by the power dynamic that plays out during a divorce.

In order to steer clear of a narcissist, or even someone with narcissistic tendencies, you first must understand how to define narcissism. Narcissism is a personality disorder in which one possesses an inflated sense of self-importance. Narcissists may believe they are superior to others and deserve special treatment. They may feel the rules do not apply to them. Narcissists may be charming and try to impress or please you. This is typically a form of manipulation or control. Their needs come first. Eventually, when you are no longer impressed or pleased, the narcissist will lash out. Narcissists often lack empathy, although their charm and manipulation may initially make them appear empathetic. They need and thrive off admiration. They also tend to be somewhat arrogant. Narcissism is a spectrum, meaning these traits are more egregious in some than in others. Interestingly, narcissism is believed to be more prevalent among men—although I have certainly encountered female narcissists.

The difficulty in identifying a narcissist is that many of the negative traits do not express themselves until you have crossed the narcissist. Of course, when you are dating, you will not necessarily see your partner's bad side. Your partner is only showing you his or her best self. Narcissists are so often charming and charismatic that they can be extremely alluring.

A narcissist also seemingly derives validation from putting you up on a pedestal in the relationship. They can pat themselves on the back for being so doting, so generous, so kind. The narcissist wins your adulation by showering you with flattery, attention, gifts, and other spoils. He or she wants you to worship them. And you will. The incentive for all this attention is *not* to make *you* feel good. The narcissist dotes on you to laud himself or herself. The more he or she adores you, the more the narcissist is adored in return. The moment you stop exalting the narcissist is the moment you witness his or her true colors. If that point happens to reveal itself to you when you are still dating, RUN! Quite often, though, it does not occur until you have a child together. We will address the way children impact a relationship with a narcissist, in the chapter "Children: The Marriage Truth Serum." Right now, we want to prevent you from getting to that point. The goal is to use the job interview to establish whether your partner possesses narcissistic tendencies.

Ironically, the reason identifying a narcissist is so difficult is the same reason falling in love with one is so easy. Narcissists are extraordinarily charming. The fact that a narcissist is either interested in or is actually dating you means the narcissist feels you are good for his or her image. A narcissist wants nothing more than for others to think he or she is as important as he or she thinks he or she is. A narcissist will put you up on a pedestal and make you feel incredibly attractive and special. No, not every would-be partner who makes you feel attractive and special is a narcissist. Your partner should make you feel attractive and special. The difference is, narcissists are *not* doing this because they feel you are attractive and special, but because you make *them* feel more attractive and special. This is distinguishable from the partner who genuinely finds you to be attractive and special and, therefore, performs gestures that make you feel attractive and special.

When a meaningful partner and a narcissist can both make you feel attractive and special, it is little wonder so many people end up in dysfunctional relationships with narcissists. It may be difficult to differentiate between one who is well intentioned and one who is not. Their outward actions and conduct appear identical. However, the purpose of the job interview is not to draw conclusions based on appearances alone. The job interview is a methodical and intellectual pursuit, calculated to dig beneath the surface—to extract specific information that might not otherwise be apparent. The job interview requires us to approach dating with critical discernment, often divorcing ourselves from our infatuation with this new, exciting relationship.

This can be extraordinarily difficult. You feel that tingling sensation every time your phone dings, hoping it's that person you are totally enamored with. Every time you are together, you gaze longingly into this person's eyes, praying he or she will finally kiss you. You think of the hug this person gave you last night as you psychotically smell the scent of his or her cologne or perfume on your sweater. The bottom line is that you are not thinking rationally. Your brain is operating on primal instincts and emotions. These sensations are so strong. They are biological. Your raging hormones and primordial drive to mate and procreate cast a spell. But you *do* have the power to shake yourself out of this stupor and ask yourself some important questions. We will talk about this more in the next chapter, "Yummy, Yummy, Yummy, I Got Love in My Tummy." For now, I touch upon it to emphasize how essential it is to detach yourself from the lust and infatuation, so that you are in a position to rationally conduct the job interview.

When your exceedingly charming and charismatic date makes you feel super attractive and special, fight the urge to swoon. Instead, use the job interview to detect whether this person may possibly be a narcissist. Stay alert. Shake yourself out of your lovestruck stupor.

There is no foolproof way to identify a narcissist. Familiarizing yourself with the characteristics of a narcissist is a good place to start. As a reminder, the job interview does not exclusively entail asking questions. The job interview includes paying attention, making observations, and analyzing and synthesizing the information you glean from your sleuthing. Is your date or partner shy and reserved, or is he or she confident? Does he or she have a big ego? When you are at a social gathering, does this person show you off to others like you're a prize? Do others in the room seem to gravitate toward this person? Is this person overly focused on your physical appearance, or does he or she acknowledge your intelligence, your kindness, and your other nonphysical attributes? Do you feel you can unabashedly be yourself around this person? If you are a person who wears makeup, do you feel comfortable being around this person without makeup on? Sure, in the start of the relationship, we all try to impress and look our best. Trust your intuition. Do you feel this person will still desire you when you throw on a pair of sweatpants, go makeup free and flaunt your unshaven legs? Is this person successful in his or her career? How does he or she treat others who upset him or her? During his or her childhood, was he or she excessively praised by his or her parent or parents?

No single answer to these questions is dispositive of whether or not someone is a narcissist. However, each offers a clue. We know that a narcissist has an inflated sense of self-importance. You may perceive this as confidence and be attracted to it. Does this confidence border on an inflated sense of self-importance? Does this person lack empathy in his or her interactions with others? Does he or she thrive off of the attention of others?

So many times, we see the signs. We just don't want to admit to ourselves that the person with whom we are so enamored may be the very thing we need to stay away from. It's kind of like chocolate cake. It tastes good. It makes you feel good. You love it. You want to eat it all the time. If you did, you would get really sick. This knowledge keeps you from eating chocolate cake all day long. Yet, you stay with the narcissist because he or she makes you feel good.

When we love someone, we convince ourselves of the reasons we should stay, rather than admit the reasons we should leave. We know that when we give up something we love, we experience negative emotions, such as sadness, loss, or grief. The good news is that these emotions are typically fleeting. You will get over it. The same cannot be said about divorcing a narcissist. The damage this divorce will do to you and your future children will likely negatively impact and in many ways destroy your life.

Chapter 6:
Yummy, Yummy, Yummy, I Got Love in My Tummy

"There is always some madness in love.
But there is always some reason in madness."
—Friedrich Nietzsche

We have all felt it. A notification pops up on your phone. Your heart pounds in your chest, hoping it's that person you met at that bar last night, who you cannot believe loves neo-psychedelia as much as you do. You've never met anyone who even knew what neo-psychedelia was! You have so much in common! It's destiny. This is definitely your soulmate—THE one.

WRONG. We have already established that mutual *superficial* interests do not equate to shared *fundamental* values. (Good. You're learning.) There is little more exciting than that first kiss you have been hoping and waiting for. Your skin tingles. You don't know whether you are going to spontaneously laugh or vomit—or both . . . simultaneously. You cannot focus. You basically lose all function of your Prefrontal Cortex waiting for the name of your "soulmate" to appear across the screen of your phone. Yes, butterflies are a wonderful feeling. But butterflies cloud the intuition. Those nefarious creatures obstruct all cognitive function, obliterating our ability to reason.

In my experience, intelligence and objectivity are not safely returned until those marauding butterflies have disappeared. That is not to say that one cannot feel butterflies in a meaningful relationship.

Generally, butterflies are intrinsic to the infatuation stage—that stage when even one's faults are perceived as endearing attributes.

In referring to his soon-to-be-ex-wife, a client once said to me: "I used to find it cute when she would get tipsy." The couple was divorcing because, many years later, the wife—who had always been an alcoholic—would get wasted and beat up the couple's children. Ultimately, the children were removed from the wife's custody. The wife did not develop an alcohol problem during the marriage. My client *chose* to perceive full-blown alcoholism as "cute" when he and his wife were dating. He was infatuated. Your mind can truly justify anything it wants to believe.

Butterflies are the rose-colored lenses that handicap our judgment. It's like those cartoon characters who fall into a trance. Their hypnotic gaze is demarcated by spiraling eyes. When you are infatuated, you are transfixed. You can't help it. Human beings are driven by their primordial urge to procreate. The survival of our species depends on it. Thus, it comes as little surprise that our urge to mate casts such a hypnotic spell over us. We've all seen those nature documentaries where the male birds ruffle their feathers performing a mating dance for the unimpressed female onlookers. The male birds strut their sweet dance moves, hoping to win the procreation lottery. When humans do this, we call it "peacocking." We're no better than those birds. Everything we do to impress a would-be mate is biologically motivated by our primal need to reproduce. The influence these forces have over us is too powerful to withstand, unless, of course, we remind ourselves that we are being held captive by them. The moment we recognize this is the moment our eyes stop spiraling—interrupting our hormone-induced stupor—and restoring our ability to reason.

We don't fail to see red flags. Those butterflies interfere, holding us back from shouting: "*This* is a fucking red flag!" I repeatedly watch perfectly intelligent people come up with excuses for unmistakable red flags that should have sent them running. Of course, when they are going through a divorce, they readily admit that they saw these red flags all along. You know a red flag when you see one. You do. Don't bury your head in the sand and refuse to acknowledge it. Eventually, that red flag will wrap its hands around your neck, pull your head out from its hiding place and force you to stare it right in the eyes.

I get it. When we identify the red flag, we know we should end the relationship. Accordingly, we instead opt to avoid designating something a red flag, excusing ourselves from taking the yucky step that must invariably follow. Justifying the reasons our partner behaves in a particular way is far more palatable than recognizing he or she may not be the right life partner. The things we love about this person are simply so wonderful. We convince ourselves, "I can totally live with *that*." We blissfully avoid the red flag designation. We tell ourselves: "I can fix that." "Oh, that's not really that bad." "That was just a one-time thing." "He doesn't usually do that." "She's working on it." "She's trying." "He doesn't really mean to act that way."

So many divorcing clients have asked me: "Next time, how can I trust myself to choose the right partner? I have been wrong before." You were not wrong. You merely chose to ignore your intuition. Remember when Pinocchio refused to listen to Jiminy Cricket, he was captured by the iniquitous Stromboli. We all have a Jiminy Cricket. Like Pinocchio, we opt not to listen and end up trapped in a cage.

One of my favorite questions to ask friends who come to me for relationship advice is this: "If I asked you the same question you are asking me, what would *you* tell me?" Routinely, my friends will respond to this question: "I would probably tell you to end the relationship."

You know the answer! Do they end the relationship? Nope. They actually tell me what they know they should do, but they don't do it. What is the reason?

Why do we press the mute button when our intuition gives us an answer we don't want to hear? Simple. Fear.

Chapter 7:
Have No Fear, Your Intelligence Is Here

"I learned that courage was not the absence of fear,
but the triumph over it. The brave man is not he who
does not feel afraid, but he who conquers that fear."
—Nelson Mandela

In the most simplistic and rudimentary sense, fear is the number one reason virtually *all* relationships fail.

The prolific Buddhist monk Thich Nhat Hanh said, "People have a hard time letting go of their suffering. Out of a fear of the unknown, they prefer suffering that is familiar." Ding, ding, ding! Fear is so powerful that it's able to persuade people to *choose* suffering over happiness. I did.

You see, each and every one of us possesses an inner voice—an innate intelligence, a Jiminy Cricket—guiding and protecting us. Unfortunately, so many of us (approximately 50 percent, to be exact) choose to ignore this voice. Surely, to do so is far easier than to listen to it. Listening to that inner voice could mean we must end a relationship we intuitively know is wrong, or at least not good enough. To listen to this voice would mean we say "no" to a second date with someone who is "so funny" and "ridiculously hot." We pacify our inner voice to justify staying in the wrong relationship. That tiny pile of red flags we have swept under the proverbial rug for so long eventually swells into an inexorable mound, as we naively stand beside it, broom in hand, continuing to sweep.

Seeking companionship is human nature. We don't want to be alone. We go to see a movie. We want to discuss it with someone. We have a bad day. We want to come home to someone who will comfort us. We want someone to cuddle in bed on a lazy Sunday morning or before we go to sleep at night. We want someone who will go and try that new restaurant with us. Yes, being alone can really suck. It can suck a hell-of-a-lot more to be with someone whose red flags you are constantly rationalizing and putting up with, purely to have someone who will embark on that ever-so-epic task of rewatching *Game of Thrones* with you from start to finish. And, you know what sucks even more than all of that? Squandering your savings to pay a divorce attorney or, worse yet, dragging your children through a contentious and acrimonious custody battle.

I would venture to say that at least 70 percent of my clients say something like, "If I knew how difficult it was to get divorced, I never would have gotten married." Marriage is not the problem. Hopefully, by picking the *right* partner, we will never know how painful, difficult, and expensive divorce can be—and that is *exactly* the reason I have written this book. **Divorce, or at the very least, a life of deep unhappiness, is almost inevitable if we choose our partner for the *wrong* reasons and, in turn, choose the *wrong* partner.** We dispense with delayed gratification in favor of instant gratification.

We ask ourselves, "What if I never meet someone like this again?" "What if I am alone forever?" "What if I am throwing away the best thing that ever happened to me?" We tell ourselves, "I've never met anyone like this before, so I will never meet anyone like this again." Such mental gymnastics only intensify our fears. We convince ourselves to stay, as the prospect of answering "yes" to any of these questions is too paralyzing to do what we instinctively know we *should* do.

One of the most prolific philosophers, Jiddu Krishnamurti, said: "Using another as a means of satisfaction and security is not love. Love is never security; love is a state in which there is no desire to be secure; it is a state of vulnerability."

If the desire for security is the fear of its absence, then it stands to reason that, at its very essence, a healthy and meaningful love is the absence of fear. By entering or remaining in a relationship out of fear of solitude or fear that you may never find someone better, you are entering or remaining in a relationship out of the desire to be secure. That is not love. That is fear. You are in this relationship for the *wrong* reason and therefore, the relationship will be wrong. You are not with your partner because you share fundamental values and want the same things for your future. You are with your partner because you are afraid to be alone. That means *you* did not select your partner. Fear selected your partner for you. Your motives for choosing the person with whom you will spend your life are flawed, which will result in you attracting a flawed relationship.

Fear manifests itself in many different ways. Yet, fear always compels people to seek out the wrong relationships and keeps them trapped in them. In my practice, fear routinely manifests in several predominant patterns. While these are not the sole ways fear manifests itself in relationships, these are some of the most prevalent ways it does. I will discuss each, in the hope that you learn to recognize these patterns, and not fall prey to them:

- **The Schedule**
- **Abuse**
- **Financial**
- **Complacency and the Unknown**
- **I Don't Want to Hurt You**

❤ The Schedule

Many of my female clients have admitted to seeing red flags in their relationships. They decided to get married anyway, as they had a "schedule." For example, a wife, let's call her Katie, met her husband, let's call him Sean, when she was twenty-seven. Katie wanted to get married by twenty-nine. She wanted to have her first child by thirty-one. Katie and Sean were never very sexually compatible. She enjoyed sex. He could take it or leave it. She liked to go out and drink. Sean's mother was an alcoholic and he was adamantly opposed to drinking. Katie went out with her girlfriends and got drunk behind Sean's back, deliberately concealing it from him. She thought, "What he doesn't know won't hurt him." Sean *did* know. He smelled it in her breath when she returned home from a girls night. It upset him. They never talked about it. They swept it all under that insidious rug. Both of them silenced their respective inner voices, hoping everything would work itself out.

When Katie turned twenty-nine, she and Sean got married. Sean just happened to be the person Katie was dating at the age she had always planned to get married. Sean fit into the schedule. Now, Katie is thirty-five. She and Sean have three children. There is no intimacy. In fact, they sleep in separate bedrooms. Katie continues to drink behind Sean's back. He resents her for it but says nothing. Katie resents Sean for judging her. She wants a divorce. She is too afraid to take that step. She doesn't want to spend any time away from her children. She isn't sure she can support herself. They stay together. The resentment grows. They ignore it, sweep, sweep, sweeping their issues under that notorious rug until the pile of dirt grows so large that they start tripping over it. They can no longer avoid their problems.

Katie ended up in my office. She and Sean ultimately got divorced. She was not wrong for drinking. He was not wrong for disapproving of drinking. They *were* wrong for each other.

Abuse

I have represented countless victims of domestic violence. The nature of abuse is such that it is not only physical, but psychological. An abuser may say things like, "Go ahead and leave. Where would you go? Who would want you?" An abuser may say these things because in reality, the abuser is *afraid* that his or her spouse will leave. The abuser will use fearmongering to make his or her victim feel so insignificant that the victim is too scared to leave the relationship. The threats can be as egregious as, "If you leave, I will take the children and you will never see them again," or "If you ever divorce me, I will kill you."

While having sought and obtained countless restraining orders on behalf of victims of domestic violence, I would never defend the actions of an abuser. I will note that, ironically, abuse is usually perpetrated by one who is, himself or herself, afraid. Deep down inside, the abuser is insecure and scared to be alone. The abuser fears that he or she is undeserving of his or her partner or that he or she is unworthy of his or her partner's love. The abuser believes he or she will never find anyone as wonderful as his or her partner. The abuser makes his or her partner feel so worthless that the partner grows too terrified to leave the abuser. Abuse is an objectively wrong way to show love. Nonetheless, it is the ugly biproduct of a person who, at his or her core, is afraid.

Of course, the victim of domestic violence is rightfully afraid the abuser will act on his or her threats. Having been subjugated for so long, the victim of domestic violence chooses to stay in the abusive relationship out of fear.

Both the abuser and the victim are afraid for different reasons. Fear keeps them both trapped in this vicious cycle.

Financial

Fear may also be financial in nature. As is often the case, one spouse may be in control of all the finances. The other spouse feels he or she cannot leave the marriage. He or she is financially unable to do so.

A scenario I repeatedly encounter is one in which the wife has given up her career to raise the children. Prior to the parties' marriage, the wife had a fulfilling career. Her husband is successful, and in a position to support the family. The wife gives birth to their first child. The couple mutually decides they would much rather the wife raise the children—as opposed to a stranger. The cost of a nanny is more than the wife is earning anyway. The couple then has another child.

Eventually, the children grow to be school-aged and the wife no longer needs to stay at home to care for them. She does not return to work. She does not need to work. The husband's income is more than sufficient to support the entire family. And, even if the wife wanted to work, she thinks, "Who would hire me? I've been out of the work force for ten years." The wife grows increasingly bored. She finds things to fill her spare time, such as going shopping, going to the hair salon, getting her nails done, and going to Pilates class. The husband grows to be resentful that his wife is "not contributing." The wife feels unfulfilled. She feels her husband does not respect her. She starts taking antidepressants. The couple has now been married for thirteen years. The wife wants to leave, but she hasn't worked in ten years and does not believe she can support herself and the children, so she chooses to stay in an unhappy marriage, popping Xanax and Klonopin to numb her misery. This is preferable to facing the scary question: "How will I support myself if I leave the marriage?"

This scenario seems cliché for good reason. It is. This is not to say that all relationships fail where one parent stays home to raise the children and the other goes to work. When a couple shares several fundamental values, communicates effectively, and both partners mutually respect one another, this will not likely be the case.

Complacency and the Unknown

Another reason people are afraid to leave a relationship is that they feel stuck or complacent. You and your partner have been dating for five years. You live together. Things are going well. In fact, "fine" is the adjective you so enthusiastically use to describe the relationship. You're not sure this is what you want for the rest of your life. Perhaps this is the reason that, after five years together, you still haven't had the urge to get engaged. You love your partner. You care deeply for him or her. You don't want to hurt your partner's feelings. But you yearn for more from a *life* partner. Maybe you recognize that, compatible though you may be, your fundamental values are different, and the foundation is not as solid as you would ideally hope. Perhaps you are afraid you won't find anyone better, even though you know this person may not be the best. There are cracks in the relationship. But you remain in it. It is easier to do so, and certainly less terrifying than leaving it.

You decide to propose. Hey, you've been together for so long, you're thirty-five years old, and splitting up the furniture you bought together after a fun-filled Sunday afternoon at IKEA seems too formidable a task. You cannot possibly bear the thought of parting with that Söderhamn sectional. It's just so comfy.

If I told you with 99 percent certainty that this marriage would be a deeply unhappy one that would end in divorce, and that the divorce would cost at least fifteen-thousand dollars, dividing the Förnuft and the Rättvik wouldn't seem like such a daunting task, right?

Maybe you could spring for another Söderhamn sectional for far less than the financial and emotional cost of a divorce ten years down the road. And yes, I have actually had clients fight over who gets to keep the sofa, so better to figure that out now, no? There will always be a piece of furniture that you don't want to divide, or an upcoming vacation that you've planned, or concert tickets that you will conveniently use to justify staying in the relationship for another day, week, or month. There will always be something to excuse you from making the unappetizing decision to end your relationship.

I Don't Want to Hurt You

Maybe you're afraid to hurt your partner. "She is so, so kind and sensitive." "He will *not* take this well." "It will destroy her." Nobody wants to hurt someone whom he or she loves. I guarantee—and I speak from personal experience—your partner *will* get over it. Time has this wonderful way of healing. Human beings are resilient. You will hurt your partner a lot more by knowingly entering a marriage, doubting its success, and ultimately ending that marriage after you have had a couple of children, bought a house, and accumulated sizable 401(k)s. You will hurt your partner a lot more when you are so deeply unhappy that you unintentionally fall in love with someone else and have an affair. It makes perfect sense, your emotional needs are not being met in your marriage—and, frankly, you were well aware those needs weren't being met before you got married.

"Who, me?" "I'd never have an affair!" I would venture to say that, with the exception of narcissists and psychopaths, most people who have an affair do not set out to do so. It happens unexpectedly, when one's needs—even beyond just sexual—are not being fulfilled.

It may start out with something as innocuous as the husband who, after the birth of the couple's second child, feels his wife no longer

acknowledges his existence. One day, at work, he strikes up an innocent conversation with a coworker. During this conversation, the husband cracks a joke. His coworker laughs. This reminds him of a time
when his wife would laugh at his silly jokes. He loved his wife's smile
and loved even more that he was the one who made her smile. While
the husband's coworker has no ulterior motive, her laugh fills a void in
his life. His coworker's laugh becomes more powerful and meaningful
than it should because the husband so desperately craves this reaction
from his wife. Like a drug, the coworker's laugh acts as the fix the husband needs to feel happy. He wants it again and he knows all he needs
do to elicit it is to crack another joke—so he does. One laugh, and then
another, leads to an intimacy between the husband and his coworker.

Afraid to go through the pain of a breakup and afraid to be alone,
we choose not to end our relationship right *now*. And yet, what happens when you go through a divorce? You go through a breakup, after
which, at least temporarily, you are alone. Except, divorce not only
comes at a tremendous emotional expense, it also carries with it a
hefty price tag. Put another way, if you were diagnosed with a disease
that will surely worsen with time, would you delay treatment? No. Of
course not. You know that, as the disease progresses, the treatment will
become more invasive, it will take longer to heal, you may experience
more suffering, and the cost of treatment will also invariably increase.

To illustrate the power of fear, I share patterns I routinely encounter
in which people stay in relationships they are otherwise too afraid to
leave. I am not here to talk about the reasons people stay in relationships. That is a book unto itself. We are talking about the patterns to
avoid so that you do not form a marriage, or even a relationship, that
will almost inevitably fail.

When fear is so powerful that it causes us to stay in relationships we know to be wrong, how do we combat it? How do we avoid these patterns and triumph over something that exerts such paralyzing control over us? If 99 percent of the people who walk through my door objectively identified their fears and refused to give into them, I would be out of a job. I cannot make you unafraid. I can, however, help you face your fears.

I remember the night my ex-husband and I separated. I felt like I wanted to press the "undo" button but couldn't find it in the task bar. I felt like I was standing outside of my own body, watching myself from across the room. I felt like I was dreaming. I thought I would wake up and realize it had all been a horrible nightmare. A few weeks later, I had dinner with a good friend. He knew that prior to meeting my ex-husband at the ripe age of seventeen, I had only casually dated. I had never been in a serious relationship. I married my first love.

At twenty-seven, I was single for the first time in my adult life. That night, I confided in my friend, "I'm afraid I will never meet anyone like my ex-husband again. We shared such a special connection." In what was oddly both a terrifying and reassuring statement, my friend told me: "You won't." He explained that I will "never have a relationship like this one ever again." He said, "Every relationship is different," promising, "you will have an equally fulfilling relationship. You will never have the *same* relationship. No two relationships are the same." In some way, it was liberating to know. I took solace in the fact that a different, albeit equally good or better relationship *could* exist. I had permission to seek something different, instead of embarking upon the impossible journey to find the same.

It took several years of dating thereafter to understand what he meant. My fear of uncertainty kept me from leaving my relationship with my ex-husband. I had to leave that relationship to realize that there was a partner better suited for me—one who could not be any more different from the former. And that is not to say my relationship with my ex-husband was bad. It was that it was not right for me. I could not admit this when I was in the relationship. I was so afraid that I would never meet anyone else with whom I felt a connection or with whom I could let myself be vulnerable. Had I been willing to face my fear early on in the relationship and admit to myself that my ex-husband and I were lacking in shared fundamental values (something I always intuitively knew), I would have ended the relationship long before we ever married. I was too afraid to do so.

I told my Jiminy Cricket to "Shut up and go away!" I muted my inner voice. I knew that if I listened to it, I had only one option, and that was to end the relationship. Instead, I made excuses and focused on the positive. I discounted the negative, constantly justifying the myriad of reasons this relationship was the right one for me. To admit otherwise was far too scary. Sound familiar? It should. This pattern is so prevalent that it's become a sad allegory.

Dating is hard. Finding a partner who suits you is not easy. Persuading yourself that someone's "right" is significantly simpler than rejecting someone with whom you are only *superficially* compatible. It's called settling. You would never settle, right? You would never pour your life's savings into a home you hated, even though you could always move, right? You would never stay at a job where you were treated poorly, even though you could always switch jobs, right? However, when marriage is presumably "'til death do you part," you settle for red flags. You are too afraid that you will never find anyone else, or that you will not make your self-imposed schedule, or that you may end up alone, or that you may be throwing away the best thing to ever happen to you in the search of something better that may not even exist.

Guess what? Right now, a wonderful woman is sitting on her couch. She is rewatching one of your favorite movies for the twelfth time, quoting along with it. It's her favorite movie too. The movie ends. She gets up, turns off the TV and heads toward her bedroom to go to sleep, but not before looking around the room and wondering, "Will I ever meet someone who will sit here and laugh at this movie with me?" "Will I ever meet someone who will cuddle on the couch with me at night after a long day?"

Right now, there is a kind man sitting at his cubicle answering work emails. He briefly pauses from his mundane routine to scroll through his social media feed. A photo pops up of his best friend from high school, pictured grinning from ear to ear. Beneath the photo, the caption reads, "She said yes. Can't wait to spend the rest of my life with my soulmate." Glancing out that sliver of window visible beyond his cubicle, the man wonders, "Will I ever find *my* soulmate?" "What will this soulmate look like?" "Where will I meet this person?" "If my soulmate is exiting the train I am getting onto, will I recognize him or her?" He longs to also find and spend the rest of his life with *his* soulmate. He just hasn't found this person yet and isn't sure he ever will. Like you, this woman and this man are asking the very same questions. They are filled with the same fears and doubts as you.

The thing is, this woman or this man may be your perfect match. The person who is meant for you *is* out there. And one day, you will be ordering a cup of coffee, or at a concert, or at a meeting, or at a party, or at a social gathering, or commuting to work, or at a sporting event, or even perusing a dating site, and that person *will* be there. You will strike up a conversation, totally unaware that three years from this moment, you will be standing across from this person, holding hands and vowing, "I do"—*not* because you *need* to get married, but because you need to get married to *this* person. You share so many fundamental values, and your relationship is built on a solid foundation. You were meant to spend your lives together.

It's interesting. Fear is something we learn. When we are born, our fears are relatively minimal. We have all seen a wobbly toddler running around—you know, the one who looks like he is about to lose his footing and take a nasty spill. He has no fear. He has never fallen before. He doesn't know that when he falls, it will hurt, so he doesn't fear it. His parents frantically chase him around, with arms extended, lunging at him every time he stumbles. They know pain. They have experienced it themselves. They want to protect him from ever experiencing it too. Eventually, the child falls. He skins his knee and cries. Afraid of replicating this pain, he learns to avoid what caused it. Next time he walks, he does so more gingerly, with a degree of apprehension.

Fear truly can be our greatest teacher. We learn to trust fear. And we *should* trust it. Fear can save, and likely has saved our lives. The fact that it has done so in the past is precisely the reason we trust everything fear tells us. It is our hero. We wouldn't jump into shark-infested waters. We are afraid to get bitten. We wouldn't touch a hot stove. We are afraid to burn ourselves. When fear has protected us for our entire lives, why would we suddenly question it? Fear has kept us alive, yet along I come telling you to reject the very benefactor that has always protected you. How do we reconcile this ostensible paradox?

Fear clamorously yells into our ear, "If you end this relationship, you will experience pain. You will be alone. You don't want to be alone, do you?" We convince ourselves, "Fear is my friend. Fear wouldn't steer me wrong." Fear is doing its job. It is protecting *present* me from experiencing pain right *now*. Here's the thing, though—fear couldn't care less about *future* you. Fear is transitory. It is your body's means of self-preservation *right now*, like your sympathetic nervous system's "fight or flight" response in stressful situations. Fear is a *short-term* defense mechanism.

Knowing that fear is only concerned with preserving you *right now*, you cannot rely on it to protect you in the future. Fear again whispers in your ear, "What if you never find someone else?" "What if you're alone forever?" Fear throws these questions at you in that precise moment you contemplate ending your relationship. If you have mustered the fortitude to say, "F-you, fear!" and end the relationship, then fear will come up with new questions, like, "What if this person is the best thing that will ever happen to you?" "What if you don't find someone by the time you're thirty-eight and you miss your window to have children?" You can't be mad at fear. It's trying to protect you. It doesn't want you to feel pain. But it doesn't quite understand.

While fear is strictly looking out for *present* you, your intelligence—your Jiminy Cricket—is looking out for both present *and* future you. Fear and intelligence are the allegorical Psychomachia—the devil and angel on opposite shoulders, battling for your attention. In the context of relationships, intelligence is the angel. The word "intelligence" comes from the Latin words "inter" meaning "between," and "legere" meaning "choose." The Latin word "intelligere" means "to understand." Our intelligence, by its very definition, imbues within us the innate power to "choose between." If we have the power to choose between, then there are *at least two options*. The choice is not made for us. We have a choice.

The word "fear" comes from the old English words "faer" meaning "calamity" or "danger," and "faeran" meaning "frighten." The word's very etymology suggests that its function is to warn you in the face of *immediate* danger, not long-term danger. It stands to reason that fear is exclusively intended to serve you in that instantaneous moment of danger. Fear strips you of your power to choose. There is just *one* option, and that option is to do exactly as fear demands. Intelligence, on the other hand, empowers us *to understand* the greater implications and consequences of our choices and actually gives us the incredible capacity to make educated decisions.

The choice to stay with someone should not be motivated by fear, but one driven by intellect. Fear does not care about future you. It doesn't. Yet *future* you is the one who must live with the choices *present* you makes. Intelligence must intervene on behalf of future you. When you ask yourself—*truly* ask yourself—am I in this relationship because I am afraid to leave it, can you give yourself the *honest* answer? If I asked you the same question you are asking me, what advice would *you* give *me*?

Chapter 8:
Don't Settle

ettling is another manifestation of fear. We settle out of fear—fear that we're not good enough or fear we may not find someone better. The pervasive sentiment "What if I don't find someone else?" sadly underscores the extent to which we diminish our value. It profoundly impacts our relationship choices. We convince ourselves that our partner is the lone person who could ever love us for who we are.

How very sad that we don't genuinely believe ourselves to be worthy of being loved. We stay in relationships, even when deep down inside, we know we shouldn't. "She's the best I have ever found" does not mean that there is not someone better suited for you. It means you haven't looked hard enough or you haven't looked long enough. Christopher Columbus didn't know America existed until he accidentally stumbled upon it. By resigning yourself to dating someone because you have "looked for so long" and were "not able to find anyone else," then, *by your own admission*, you are settling. In professing you have been unable to find anyone *better*, you are conceding that this person may not be the best, or even good enough. This person is merely "enough." This doesn't mean you set unattainable standards. Set high standards. If the person you choose to marry is the most important decision you will ever make in your life, why would you so easily give up on your quest to find the *right* person? Why would you settle?

I once represented a woman, let's call her Joan, who had married her husband, let's call him Tyler, after they had been together for five years. Joan was incredibly close to her mother and her two siblings. Tyler would deliberately avoid spending time with Joan's family. It made him uncomfortable. Joan would excuse his behavior, telling herself: "He's just really shy. We are working on it." She would make excuses for Tyler, such as: "His father left when he was young. He's afraid to meet new people. He will come out of his shell." What amazing and wonderful qualities could Tyler have possessed that made Tyler's behavior acceptable to Joan? Incidentally, Tyler did enjoy spending time with his own family and frequently asked Joan to spend time with them—which, as someone who fundamentally valued family, Joan happily did. Joan grew to resent Tyler. Joan believed Tyler would change. When she married Tyler, Joan was aware of his flaws. Joan concocted excuses for Tyler's behavior, so that she would not be forced to break up with him and ultimately be alone. She merely delayed the inevitable, subjecting herself to far worse pain than she would have experienced had she ended the relationship when she and Tyler were dating. Joan settled. As a result, she was faced with two choices: 1) stay in a miserable relationship, or 2) get divorced. She opted for the latter, which was inevitable given Joan married Tyler for the wrong reasons.

Joan used Tyler's childhood traumas and experiences to justify his otherwise objectionable behavior. By empathizing with Tyler, Joan convinced herself to stay in a relationship with him while completely overlooking the fact that his red flags should have been deal breakers. Joan's fear of being alone or potentially never finding someone "better" than Tyler proved so powerful that she was willing to swallow a bitter pill. When Joan accepted Tyler's behavior, that bitter pill forever lodged itself in her throat—an inescapable reminder of her decision to settle.

Although you should always have compassion for your partner and understand that your partner's past is part of the delicate fabric of his or her emotional and psychological makeup, you must simultaneously be cautious not to conflate compassion with settling. *Understanding the origin of a person's dysfunctional behavior may help to engender compassion for him or her. That compassion should not be used to excuse and accept this person's dysfunctional behavior.* You can have empathy for someone and still refuse to endure his or her dysfunctional behavior for the rest of your life. Joan mistook acceptance for compassion. The two are not mutually exclusive. You can understand where someone is coming from. You can approach a person with sensitivity and empathy. That does not mean you should accept his or her unacceptable behavior for the rest of your life and hope it will get better. Yes, there are exceptions to every rule. For the most part though, behaviors get worse as we grow increasingly comfortable in relationships. They do not typically "get better."

Of course, no person is without a past. Every single human being is a product of his or her emotional wounds and life experiences—good and bad. In many ways, our deepest traumas shape us and our relationship to the world. When we choose to self-reflect and use our hurt for personal growth, that hurt has the power to breed tremendous beauty and strength. The fact is, when you feel the incessant need to justify your partner's behavior, he or she is not the right partner for you. You may have empathy for what led your partner to behave in a certain way. But if that behavior does not meet your standards, then regardless of your compassion for your partner, you must end the relationship.

As we have established, you and your partner are a team. A team is only as good as its individual players. When one player is injured, the team suffers. Your marital partner is not a project. Your husband or wife is your cocaptain, your equal, your partner in life. While at times you may need to carry your partner through an illness, job loss, disability, or any other curve ball life will invariably throw your way, this is not the same as entering a marriage while already carrying your partner on your back. Eventually, he or she will get heavy, you will get tired, and you will need him or her to get off so you can rest and recover.

Joan overlooked the fact that Tyler avoided her family. She knew that Tyler had what she characterized as a "difficult childhood." Having compassion and empathy for others is important. Equally, if not more important, is having compassion for yourself. You may equate companionship with happiness. Yet, ironically, by choosing companionship with the wrong person, you assure yourself a life of deep unhappiness. A life spent making excuses for your partner's behavior is exhausting at best. You persuade yourself that enduring your partner's behaviors in the name of patience and understanding deems you worthy of canonization. Ultimately, when you file for divorce, the very person to whom you touted yourself for showing compassion will feel sad. So, is your decision to settle truly compassionate—or is it actually selfish?

Joan deluded herself into believing that her love for Tyler warranted tolerating his behavior. In reality, Joan stomached Tyler's behavior because she didn't want to be alone. If Joan truly loved Tyler, she wouldn't have tolerated him. She would have revered him. Joan's fear of being alone did both her and Tyler a great disservice. Joan did not feel she deserved better or, perhaps she was afraid she would not find better. She would often say, "I can be a very difficult person" as though settling was justified by the fact that she—like *every single living person*—could sometimes be "difficult." She thought she had found the one person who would ever love her.

Tyler's love was so powerful that Joan was willing to ignore the fact that Tyler did not want to spend time with her family—the family to whom she was so very close. Some love was better than no love. Joan did not stop to consider that she was a kind, intelligent, successful, and funny human being whom a number of men would have considered themselves lucky to date and marry. She did not view herself this way.

As an aside, there is a difference between narcissism and self-worth. To value oneself is not an act of narcissism. It is an act of self-love. To have confidence is not the same as cockiness. Cockiness is false confidence. It stems from insecurity. Quite the contrary, confidence demonstrates security. Confidence is a good quality. To be confident is important. Valuing yourself and having high expectations for yourself is also important.

If you do not believe you deserve the absolute best, you will not have the absolute best. You may end up with the worst. Sometimes, believing you deserve the best is easier said than done. Self-love is so complex. Our perceptions of love and relationships are so interwoven with our childhood and our past experiences. The way we were shown love, if we were shown love, is the way we learn to love and be loved. I am not a psychologist. This book is not about child development or its impact on our understanding of love. I point out these concepts simply to highlight the ways our self-worth is so profoundly linked to what we believe we deserve and, consequently, the type of relationship we seek out. If you feel yourself to be undeserving of love, then prior to starting a relationship, you may wish to participate in counseling to work through those issues. Like attracts like. By starting to date in a healthy way, you will attract a healthy relationship.

One of my clients, let's call her Margot, was a highly successful, gorgeous entrepreneur. Prior to marrying her husband, let's call him Brad, Margot started and ran what eventually became a multimillion-dollar business. When Margot met Brad, he was a struggling actor, waiting tables and living paycheck to paycheck. When they were dating, Brad was incredibly kind, sweet and, in her words, "a real gentleman." He put Margot up on a pedestal—and rightfully so. Margot grew up in a privileged home. Her parents divorced when she was eight years old. Her father was extremely strict and, in some ways, contributed to Margot's low self-esteem. Brad doted over Margot and Margot was completely enchanted. She so badly wanted to be loved that she settled for someone who had little to offer her other than intense adulation.

Had Margot taken the time to do so, she would have recognized that she and Brad did not share fundamental values. Their goals in life could not have been any more different. Brad struggled with his own issues, including addiction, which he never truly resolved. Margot married Brad anyway. Over the course of their relationship, Margot deliberately sabotaged her own success, perceiving it as a threat to Brad's ego. She did not want Brad to feel that her success eclipsed his. In turn, Brad perpetually felt insecure living in the shadow of Margot's success. He felt the need to keep up, but felt he never could. Not surprisingly, the marriage failed. No matter how much Margot sacrificed her own goals to make Brad feel better about himself, Brad never felt good enough for Margot. Margot was so afraid to be alone and was so smitten by the seemingly unwavering adoration Brad provided that she married him anyway, predominantly because Brad worshiped her. Margot's fear was so powerful that it convinced her to settle for someone with whom she was incompatible. When she was divorcing Brad, I asked her whether she knew, or at least sensed that she and Brad were wrong for one another. She admitted she had always known. Knowing this in no way mitigated Margot's pain when she and Brad ended their relationship—and now, Margot was left to navigate co-parenting three children with a man who was largely incapable of taking care of himself.

My practice is a revolving door of Margots—men and women who do not perceive themselves worthy of a partner that meets certain standards; men and women so afraid to be alone that they settle.

This pattern is so prevalent that frankly, I'm bored by it. A person sabotages his or her own career and success to make his or her partner feel less inadequate. This self-sabotage stops this person from achieving his or her true potential in life, and perhaps even leads this person to eventually resent his or her partner. No matter how much one partner sabotages his or her career, the other still never feels good enough. It becomes a vicious cycle of shame, guilt, envy, and resentment that crescendos into an unstoppable avalanche. This relationship dynamic cannot work. It never works. The couple does not share fundamental values. One partner—usually the more successful of the two—enters the relationship out of fear he or she won't find anyone better. The other partner frantically scrambles to keep up.

How do you know whether you are settling? How do you avoid it? Let's do another exercise:

Exercise 5: I Deserve Better

If you have a sibling to whom you are very close, think about what qualities you would want your sibling's life partner to possess. If you don't have a sibling, think about your best friend. Write down ten qualities you would want your best friend's partner to possess.

1. _____

2. _____

3. _____

4. _____

5. _____

6. _____

7. _____

8. _____

9. _____

10. _____

Now, take a look at this list. Do you believe these are qualities you also deserve in your life partner?

If you are currently dating or in a relationship with someone, does this person possess all ten of these qualities? Be honest with yourself.

If your partner does not possess all ten of these qualities—why is that? If you do not believe yourself deserving of a partner who possesses all of these qualities, what are the reasons? By not believing you deserve better, you will not demand better. You will settle out of the need to be in a relationship, rather than holding out for the right relationship. Whether through therapy or by other means of self-evaluation, you must decipher the reason or reasons you feel you are undeserving of a mate who possesses the qualities you would want your sibling's or friend's partner to have.

You are a wonderful person who deserves to love and be loved—and in the *right* way. Why do you believe that you could not find someone else or many someone elses? Yes, finding "the one" could be like locating a needle in a haystack. The thing about the needle in the haystack is that it *is* there. If you take the time to carefully sift through the hay, you *will* find the needle. It's worth the hunt.

Chapter 9:
But They're "Nice"

"It is not enough to be nice;
you have to be good. We are
attracted by nice people; but only
on assumption that their niceness is
a sign of goodness."
—Roger Scruton

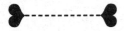

Attuning ourselves to our behaviors can clue us into their root cause. Fear often manifests itself in the form of justifications. We can convince ourselves of anything we want to believe. We excuse our partner's conduct or persuade ourselves to live with behaviors we would otherwise find unacceptable.

One of the most pervasive ways we justify staying in the wrong relationship is by telling ourselves that our partner is "so nice." "Nice" is what you say about someone who doesn't have any other admirable qualities. Okay, that may be a little harsh. The point is, "nice" is not enough. Yeah, he's nice. She's nice. A lot of people are nice. Does that mean you should marry him or her? (I'll let you go ahead and answer this one.) An applicant is rarely given the job just because he or she is "nice." The applicant must also boast an impressive resumé that qualifies him or her for the position. He or she should be nice too. Nice, in and of itself, is not enough to get the job.

Your friends like the person you're dating? Amazing! What are you waiting for? Don't walk. Run to the altar! (In case it wasn't clear, this is sarcasm.) I'll bet anything your friends value their relationship with you. I'll bet your friends don't want to do anything to jeopardize their relationship with you. I'll bet your friends will tell you they like your significant other, even when they don't. They don't want to lose you as a friend. Only the people who truly care about you are willing to tell you the truth. They don't want to see you get hurt. Do you listen? Or do you shun those who tell you what you intuitively know to be true, but don't want to hear? If you do rebuff them, why? What motive could they possibly have for confronting you, despite the fact that they know what they have to say will likely upset you and possibly alienate you from them? If you are fortunate enough to have someone in your life who cares enough about you to actually put himself or herself in this compromising position, this is likely the one person whose opinion you should consider.

Yeah, you're dating a "nice" person, whom your friends "like." This has success written all over it. (Yes, more sarcasm.) These are things I hear people say, though. It is so obvious. These reasons, although helpful in convincing *you* that someone with whom you are incompatible is right, are not good reasons to marry someone. These are ways we rationalize to ourselves that we are in the "right" relationship. Why? We are too afraid to admit we are in the *wrong* relationship. "Nice" is not enough to qualify the candidate for the job position. It most certainly isn't enough to qualify your partner for the most important job position—your spouse.

Chapter 10

The House That Foundation Built

"The loftier the building, the
Deeper must the 'foundation' be laid."
—Thomas à Kempis

Before we explore the reasons that a solid foundation is so indispensable to a relationship, we need to define what it means. The word "foundation" comes from the Latin verb "fundare," meaning "to lay a base for." In English, "foundation" means "the underlying base or support." When we talk about the foundation of a relationship, we are referring to the Pillars that support the relationship—the elements that keep it from toppling over. In order for any relationship to be successful, all five of these characteristics *must* exist, and all five must exist in *every* single relationship, regardless of each individual's unique fundamental values.

A few years ago, my husband and I were trying to buy a house. We found a property for an amazing price; one we knew would be a great investment. We made an offer. The seller accepted. We opened escrow and started the inspection process—which included a foundation inspection. During the foundation inspection, the inspector pulled back the carpet. Hidden beneath it was a giant, deep crack that ran the length of several rooms. I know little to nothing about foundations. I *did* know what I was looking at was not good. The inspector explained that the foundation was so corroded that the back half of the house was actually tearing away from its front. The house was literally sliding down the hill. To repair this was cost-prohibitive. We could not live in this house when its foundation was in such a state. Ultimately, the problems with the foundation led us to pull out of the sale.

A relationship is like a house. You need not know much about construction to know that, in order to build a house or a building, you must first build a strong foundation. Without it, whatever you build on top will invariably fall. Foundations consist of concrete, support beams, pylons, and other strong support mechanisms. You wouldn't live in a house with a dilapidated foundation. You want some assurance that, if there is an earthquake or a hurricane, your house, you, and all of the things in it will remain intact. For some reason, we do not expect the same of our relationships. We fail to demand that our relationship be built on a solid foundation so that it does not ultimately topple over like that (like, OMG) giant Jenga set you and your date played at that fun bar you went to on your second date.

We have already established the predominant difference between fundamental values and foundation. Whereas fundamental values are unique to each person and differ from relationship to relationship, the attributes that make up a solid foundation are identical in every single relationship. Fundamental values are distinguishable from foundation in other ways, though. Returning to our house analogy, whereas the foundation is the glue that holds the structure together, fundamental values are the actual land. You cannot build a house when you don't have the land to build on. Ascertaining whether your partner shares your fundamental values is the quest to find the perfect piece of land for your home. Once you find the right land, *then* you can start building. Okay—enough with the construction analogies. What I am getting at is, you cannot even begin to build a foundation with someone with whom you do not share fundamental values. Although fundamental values and foundation are distinct, they are also symbiotic. When you and your partner share fundamental values, you are far more likely to successfully build a solid foundation. Through your shared belief systems, you will approach and, therefore, resolve conflicts in a similar way.

The biggest mistake so many people make is that they try to build a solid foundation with someone with whom they do not share fundamental values. You cannot build a house without land. Take my word for it. Don't try. Move on. Kick 'em to the curb (not literally, but figuratively).

Once you have established that you and your partner *do* share fundamental values, you are now ready to build a foundation. How? What does a solid foundation look like? While there are certainly many factors, I have identified the five indispensable cornerstones of a solid foundation. I like to call them the Five Pillars. In the absence of all Five Pillars, the structure, or your relationship, cannot be supported. Often, when one Pillar falls, the others invariably come crashing down. Like support beams that hold up a house, the foundational Pillars hold up a relationship. Consistent throughout most, if not all, failed relationships is the absence of one, several, or all of these foundational Pillars:

- **Trust**
- **Honesty**
- **Communication**
- **Teamwork**
- **Respect**

Let's delve into each Pillar a little deeper.

♡ Trust

At the risk of stating the obvious, trust is a prerequisite to any relationship. This is equally true of relationships between romantic partners as it is of relationships between businesspeople, friends, and family members. Trust is the cement that fortifies your house. Without cement, your home will fall over. Without trust, your relationship will crumble.

Trust is not something we should give readily. Trust is earned. It grows over time. It develops as two people begin to let one another into each other's lives. Trust is an interesting animal. It is not until we trust our partner and begin to make ourselves vulnerable to him or her that we feel comfortable sharing our innermost secrets. At the same time, when our partner feels comfortable in exposing his or her vulnerabilities to us, we in turn trust our partner. This suggests that trust is very much a reciprocal dance. Trust is not easily earned. Once betrayed, it is instantaneously lost and scarcely ever recovered.

Many divorces are the result of an extramarital affair. For most, an affair is an instantaneous deal breaker. However, a small few make an effort to move past the infidelity. Interestingly, the word "infidelity" derives from the Latin root word "fides" meaning "loyalty" and "trust." The very etymology of the word "infidelity" itself reveals that to be unfaithful is to forsake one's trust. Not surprisingly, a couple will rarely move beyond the extramarital affair. In my experience, no matter how much the adulterous spouse is genuinely remorseful, the other will always think, "He or she hid it from me last time and I didn't know. What if he or she is hiding it from me again?" Of course, there are always exceptions. Those exceptions are few and far between.

Breaches of trust are not limited to extramarital affairs. They include lies, no matter how small or seemingly innocuous. By way of example, I have represented many people whose now former spouses were addicts. Specifically, I represented one woman, let's call her Cherie, whose husband, let's call him George, struggled with alcohol addiction. During their marriage, Cherie occasionally found bottles of alcohol hidden in various locations throughout their home—this was when George claimed to be "sober." When Cherie found the bottles, she confronted George. He insisted those bottles had been hidden long ago and that he was now sober. He swore to it. Cherie so desperately wanted to believe him that she did, until she again found bottles hidden in new places. She confronted George. And again, George swore he was sober. Except this time, Cherie no longer trusted George. After all, one does not usually hide bottles unless he is avoiding their discovery. Cherie understood deception was a symptom of addiction. She recalled her wedding vows, "for better or for worse, in sickness and in health." She reminded herself addiction is a disease. No matter how much she placated the nagging voice inside her head, Cherie could not look past the repeated betrayal. She thought to herself, "Fool me once, shame on you. Fool me twice, shame on me."

When George was finally sober, Cherie no longer trusted him. He had lied to her in the past. The previous dishonesty engendered future distrust, knocking down one of the Pillars essential to the relationship and irreparably damaging its very foundation. The ongoing distrust precipitated a bevy of corollary issues. Namely, George started to feel he was constantly under scrutiny. Even after George actually became sober, Cherie did not believe him, leading George to grow resentful of Cherie. George could not escape Cherie's perpetual questioning and distrust. That is not to say Cherie's distrust was unjustified. In fact, it was. Similarly, an adulterous spouse recommitted to saving his or her marriage cannot escape the incessant scrutiny of his or her partner, who, understandably, constantly questions the adulterous spouse's whereabouts. Every text message arouses suspicion and incites false accusations. Basically, it's virtually impossible to recover trust once it is gone.

Yes, some are able to, at least superficially, move beyond the fractured trust. Whether or not they genuinely overcome it I cannot say. Those who choose to stay in the relationship do not end up in my office. The couple's ability to transcend the distrust may depend on the strength of the remaining four foundational Pillars.

Honesty

Honesty and trust go hand in hand but are nevertheless distinguishable from one another. Trust is something that is earned—it is passive. Honesty is something that you do—it is active. When someone is honest with you, he or she gains your trust. The inverse is not necessarily true. The mere fact that one may trust you does not render you honest. Your partner's failure to be honest may lead to distrust.

Honesty is also interesting because, ostensibly, there are varying degrees of dishonesty. Benjamin Franklin once said: "Half a truth is often a great lie." One may be dishonest by omission. In the obvious example of an extramarital affair, the adulterous spouse may never deny that he or she is having an affair, unless confronted by his or her partner. The adulterous spouse is not actively telling a lie. However, he or she is being dishonest by neglecting to reveal that he or she is having intercourse with another person, when his or her partner believes and expects the adulterous spouse to be monogamous.

Omissions may be far more subtle, like in the case of a woman who really, really wants to have children. She knows her partner has no interest in having children. She believes that once she and her partner are married, she will manage to convince him that *he*, too, wants children. She treats the subject as minutia that will somehow work itself out. This woman's partner never discusses children with her, and in turn, she keeps quiet on the subject of children, biding her time until he proposes and the marriage is a done deal.

Six months into their marriage, the wife expresses to her husband how badly she wants children. The husband still has no desire to have children. The wife unrelentingly pleads with her husband. Finally, the husband gives in. The couple has their first child. After many sleepless nights, the wife asks her husband to help with the nighttime feedings. He reluctantly does, yet longs for the days when he enjoyed a night of uninterrupted sleep and could go out with his buddies any time. He starts to resent his wife for, in his mind, forcing him into a reality he did not want—although, undeniably, he was not an unwilling participant. He loves his baby. Parenthood—and all of the things that accompany it—just isn't what he wanted for his life.

The wife grows to resent her husband for being unsupportive and uninvolved. She even accuses him of "not loving" their newborn child. You get the picture. No matter how compatible these two may be, she fundamentally values parenthood. He does not. Had she been honest with him when they were dating, they could have identified that this was a fundamental value they did not share. Though they may love each other, they wanted different things for their lives. There is nothing wrong with this, other than that it may come to be an irreconcilable difference. Perhaps the husband avoided the topic altogether, hoping that by not broaching it, his wife would never bring it up. He was *also* dishonest and therefore equally culpable for not discussing a topic every single couple *must* discuss prior to marriage. The wife was so preoccupied with locking down the marriage proposal that she figured everything would magically work out in the "happily ever after." She closed her eyes and trivialized the not-so-minor details.

We know honesty and trust are the *sine qua non* of a solid relationship. But how do we know if someone is being honest or dishonest so that we know whether or not to trust them? Much to the dismay of many of my clients, my admission to the State Bar of California does not carry with it a crystal ball holding all of the secrets to the universe. I cannot tell you whether someone is lying. There are certainly a lot of very skilled liars out there, many of them narcissists or psychopaths, or psychopathic narcissists (though, at this point, you are somewhat adept at sniffing out one of those). I will venture to say that, for the most part, you intuitively know when your partner is being untruthful. The question then becomes, how badly do you want to believe what you are being told? I would venture to say that most people who are being lied to *know* they are being lied to. They simply want to believe the lie enough that they are willing to accept it at face value.

There is no better example of this than the woman who says she is on birth control. (I swear to you, this is so common, it's like a fucking bad script.) Virtually every single man who knows he is about to have intercourse with a woman *wants* to believe that woman when she says she is on birth control. In that very moment, when deciding whether to put on a condom (or maybe he doesn't have one), he prefers to trust that his partner is on birth control than to question her. I'm not talking about a one-night stand. I am talking about a person with whom this man is in a serious relationship that is (if all things work out) likely headed for marriage.

I once represented a man whose wife used the ol' "I'm on birth control" routine. It's the oldest trick in the book. The couple was not married at the time. On more than several occasions, the woman, let's call her Isabelle, had openly communicated to my client, let's call him Elliot, that she wanted to be married. Elliot never wanted to get married. Isabelle badly wanted children. In fact, she told Elliot how much she wanted a baby. Elliot had a child from a previous relationship with a woman to whom he was never married. Elliot knew how desperately

Isabelle wanted to be married and, even more so, to have children. He knew that Isabelle was approaching an age at which childbearing may no longer be possible, or at least would become much more difficult. In fact, although they had no plans to marry, to appease her, Elliot bought Isabelle a diamond ring that she wore on her left hand. Elliot never officially proposed. That didn't stop Isabelle from showing it off and telling everyone they were engaged.

After dating for about five years, one night, they had sex. Prior to doing so, Elliot actually asked Isabelle—who was, at this point, approaching forty—whether she had taken her birth control. She said yes. Several weeks later, Elliot and Isabelle learned that Isabelle was pregnant. Elliot asked Isabelle how this was possible. Elliot asked Isabelle whether she took her birth control and Isabelle assured him that she had. When Elliot confronted her, Isabelle admitted that, on this particular night, she was "drunk" and "forgot" to take the pill. Incidentally, this is the same night Elliot asked Isabelle whether she had taken her birth control. Despite Isabelle's alleged impairment, Elliot's question should have served as a sufficient reminder to her to take her birth control. Clearly, she intentionally "forgot" to take it and knew she hadn't taken it when she misrepresented to Elliot that she had. Shortly thereafter, Elliot officially proposed to Isabelle, albeit she was already sporting the ring. Before she gave birth to their daughter, they were married. A very pregnant Isabelle, with her eye on the prize, got her fairy-tale wedding. Spoiler alert: they got divorced. It was an ugly one. Like, really, really ugly. Are you surprised? I'm not. At this point, you shouldn't be either.

Let's take a step back and evaluate this situation. We know Isabelle wanted a baby more than anything. We know that she badly wanted to be married. We know that she was almost forty years old. How do we know all of these things? Isabelle told them to Elliot. She didn't hide her thoughts or feelings. Elliot just chose not to listen. Does this mean that every woman who desperately wants to be married and have a child will lie about being on birth control? Absolutely not! In this particular scenario, the night Elliot and Isabelle had intercourse, Elliot had the foresight to ask Isabelle whether she had taken her birth control. She had been on birth control for the past five years of their relationship and Elliot had never once before asked Isabelle this question prior to having intercourse. That night, something inside of Elliot prompted him to ask, suggesting he suspected there was a possibility Isabelle may *not* have taken her birth control. Had Elliot been absolutely certain Isabelle would take her birth control, he most likely would not have asked whether she had. When Isabelle responded, "yes," Elliot wanted to believe she was telling the truth, otherwise, he would have had to abstain or use protection. In that very moment, it was more convenient for him to believe that Isabelle was telling the truth than to question her or trust his instincts. How amazing that even in these moments of lust and passion, our inner voice interjects to warn us. This particular gentleman assuaged his inner voice by telling it, "I asked." He wanted to believe what Isabelle, his partner, told him. The question is, did he genuinely believe her when she assured him that she took her birth control?

Let's take a look at another example. A number of my clients share with me the ways they discover their partner is having an affair. (I'm a veritable treasure trove of juicy and salacious stories, worthy of a Jackie Collins novel.) Often, my client will shamefully admit to having "snooped" through his or her partner's phone or emails. Here's the thing, though: one does not ordinarily snoop through another's text messages or emails unless seeking confirmation of what he or she already suspects or knows to be true.

We have all seen movies depicting the cliché husband having an affair with his secretary. What does he do? He calls his wife to say he has to "work late." Maybe the husband comes home smelling of perfume. Perhaps the husband must leave town to "attend a business meeting." In this scenario, the husband is suddenly working more and working later. His behavior is different. The wife, who knows her husband well and is familiar with his work and his every mannerism, suspects her husband is having an affair. She cannot accuse her husband without proof. Surely, he will deny it and tell his wife she is "crazy." Gaslighting at its absolute finest! The wife doesn't feel right ending a thirteen-year marriage without confirmation of her suspicions. One night, when her husband is in the shower, the wife looks through her husband's recently deleted photos on his phone. She discovers a number of racy photos of the same woman, location stamped Cabo San Lucas, and dated the very weekend the husband was purportedly on a "business trip." The wife knew she was going to find something. She looked only to confirm her suspicions.

Now, I most certainly do not advocate snooping through your partner's phone. I am simply pointing out that the impetus for doing so is likely precipitated by something we already intuitively sense. In this scenario, the wife may not want to look through her husband's phone. She knows she will find something that will leave her with no choice but to end her marriage. She musters the fortitude and makes the very difficult decision to seek it out. Even if she did not snoop through her husband's phone, the fact that she felt compelled to do so might have been a sufficient indication that her husband was most likely being dishonest with her.

You will not always know that your partner is being dishonest. This book is not an instruction manual on affair or lie detection. I do, however, believe that when your partner is being dishonest, most of the time you know. Often, you refuse to admit to yourself that your partner is being untruthful. **Being oblivious to it is not the same as being**

unwilling to admit to yourself that your partner is lying. In many ways, this comes back to fear.

By acknowledging that our partner is lying, we will likely need to end the relationship. Without a doubt, this is a terrifying prospect— one that carries with it a potential slew of unpleasant repercussions. Accordingly, we ignore what our inner voice is telling us or even screaming out to us. I am here to remind you that your inner voice exists. It is your most devoted protector, and you should trust and listen to it. If your inner voice is telling you something you don't want to hear, that may be all the more reason to listen to it.

You will not always know when someone is being dishonest. But when your intuition leads you to question your partner's fidelity, it may very well be right.

Communication

It's no secret. Communication is indispensable to a successful relationship. Alas, a common theme among so many relationships that fail is poor communication, or a total lack thereof. Communication is a complex concept. Our failure to communicate and the way we communicate are equally significant.

If you fail to communicate, your partner cannot meet your needs. In turn, you deprive yourself of a fulfilling relationship, and ultimately, a fulfilling life. Your partner is left guessing what you think, asking the ever-so-infamous question, "Is something wrong?" to which you give that ubiquitous and often infuriating response: "I'm fine." Your partner is likely asking because he or she genuinely wants to know how to behave differently. Your partner possesses a sincere desire to modify his or her behavior to avoid repeating it and upsetting you in the future. Your partner is not a mind reader. Everyone is different. What upsets you may not upset your partner. By expressing to your partner the way his or her conduct made you feel, your partner can mitigate his or her behavior in the future, just as you would do the same for your partner. I am most certain that, if you were to respectfully express to your partner the way his or her actions made you feel, your partner would be receptive. Otherwise, your partner would not ask you if something was wrong to begin with. If your partner isn't receptive, he or she isn't the right partner.

So, why do we hold back? Why do we answer, "I'm fine," when really, we are far from it? One possibility is that we secretly hope our partner recognizes his or her behavior was hurtful to us. We want our partner to realize that he or she acted in an unacceptable way and immediately apologize without our prompting. This is not entirely realistic, and frankly, it is childish. Your partner is not psychic. Wonderful though that may sound, that isn't what you actually want. We all have different sensitivities and needs. You may do something totally innocuous and inadvertently hurt your partner. If your actions hurt or upset the person you love, you would want to know so you don't repeat those actions. Your partner, too, wants to know if something he or she does upsets you, so he or she will not do it again. Your partner cannot always know what caused you to be upset unless you tell him or her.

This scenario always reminds me of a scene from the movie *The Break-Up* starring Jennifer Aniston and Vince Vaughn. Jennifer Aniston and Vince Vaughn's characters are in a relationship. They live together. Jennifer Aniston's character, Brooke, is throwing a dinner party. Vince Vaughn's character, Gary, is tired after a long day of work. Brooke asks Gary to pick up twelve lemons from the store on his way home from work. Gary gets the lemons but only buys a mere three. After the guests have gone, Gary lays down on the couch. Brooke proceeds to clean. Gary doesn't offer to help. Brooke is irritated. An argument ensues. Exasperated, Brooke says to Gary, "I want you to want to do the dishes." Gary explains he is tired. Brooke reminds him that she, too, worked all day. The exchange is almost reminiscent of a mother reprimanding her oblivious eight-year-old son. The number of times Brooke and Gary have had this or a similar exchange is unclear to the audience. Yet, their mutual resentment is apparent—the visible biproduct of their respective pent-up frustration.

This scene is so well-written. It astutely captures the nuanced communication issues inherent to so many relationships. Brooke does not feel like Gary cares about her. Brooke has arrived at this conclusion through Gary's actions (presumably over time). Brooke asks Gary for a favor—to bring home twelve lemons. Gary believes that he has shown Brooke that he cares about her by bringing home any lemons at all. However, Gary brings home only three lemons, as opposed to twelve. Brooke perceives this a passive-aggressive act—as if Gary views her simple request for a small favor too burdensome. Gary doesn't stop to consider the implications of saddling Brooke with the sole responsibility of cleaning up after the dinner party. He is exhausted and wants to rest, which is understandable. Brooke is not incorrect in deeming this selfish. Gary is unwilling to inconvenience himself to help Brooke, who is tired after working all day and throwing a dinner party.

Maybe Gary didn't want to throw a dinner party. He went along with the idea because he knew it was important to Brooke. Quite possibly, Gary was annoyed that Brooke chose to throw a dinner party on a day that he worked. Rather than expressing the way he felt or asking Brooke to schedule a dinner party on a different day, Gary said nothing at all. He knew Brooke would have been upset, so he chose to keep quiet. Or possibly, Gary made it clear to Brooke that he did not want to throw a dinner party at all, and Brooke still did as she pleased. It could be that in the past, Brooke pouted or reprimanded Gary for speaking up, deterring Gary from speaking up on this occasion. Maybe Gary was simply the type of guy who never spoke up. Gary might have even agreed to the dinner party, but thought that by doing so, he was absolved from participating in the clean-up efforts. Brooke and Gary didn't express any of these thoughts to each other. Each expected the other to know what he or she was thinking.

Their final showdown wasn't about lemons or dishes. They suppressed their feelings for so long that they erupted over trivialities.

Although I suspect many of the foundational Pillars were unstable in Brooke and Gary's relationship, the communication Pillar was downright ramshackle. Brooke expected Gary to read her mind. She wanted him to *want* to do the dishes. She hoped Gary would do things that were just not Gary—essentially expecting him to be someone he wasn't. It may be that earlier in the relationship, Brooke attempted to express her frustrations to Gary. His ongoing unwillingness to behave differently ultimately caused Brooke to internalize her feelings until her resentment eventually boiled over. Gary thought he was making an effort, but never felt it was enough, so he stopped. It's possible that Gary's effort wasn't enough for Brooke. Gary wasn't right for Brooke. Spoiler alert—as the film's title suggests—Brooke and Gary do break up. The inability to communicate ruined their relationship.

At one point, Brooke and Gary likely tried to communicate. They spoke different languages and didn't quite understand one another. However, oftentimes, two people completely fail to communicate whatsoever in their relationship. Every thought and emotion is repressed, eventually bubbling up to the surface in an inevitable explosion. The predominant reason people neglect to communicate with their partners is our good old friend, that dirty F-word: Fear. We think, "What if I tell my partner how I really feel, and he or she breaks up with me?" "What if it turns into a fight? I don't want to deal with that." "What if I tell my partner how I feel, and he or she is no longer attracted to me?" Sure, it's possible your partner will break up with you. That's always possible. By that same token, why would you want to be in a relationship with someone who doesn't respect how you feel and would break up with you for it? And, if you need to conceal your feelings from your partner, then your relationship is not predicated on honesty and trust—meaning it's lacking in at least two of the Five Pillars.

Remember, your house cannot stand without a foundation. Your relationship will not last without one either. For each Pillar that is weak or lacking, your relationship is all the more likely to collapse. If you fear that by communicating, you will elicit an unwanted reaction, then perhaps intuitively you know that your partner may not be the right person for you. Your inability to express the way you feel may have something to do with your own fears and insecurities. It may also have to do with the fact that your partner is unable to communicate maturely and respectfully. At the very least, it should lend some insight into the lasting power of this relationship. Do you sense that expressing your feelings will evoke a negative response from your partner? Then it may be that your partner is unwilling to understand your needs. Your partner's needs are more important to him or her than yours. Breaking news: you should not be with this person!

The way we communicate can be just as harmful as our failure to do so. So often, I watch people get angry, when in reality, beneath that façade, they are actually hurt. Ostensibly, people associate hurt with weakness and vulnerability, while they associate anger with power and control. Afraid to show our vulnerability and express our hurt, we instead lash out. We start pointing fingers and casting aspersions, attributing motives to our partner, rather than expressing to our partner the way his or her conduct made us feel.

For example, a husband forgets his and his wife's wedding anniversary. His wife is hurt by this. She feels this means the relationship is not important to her husband. Instead of calmly and rationally expressing to her husband how his failure to remember their anniversary made her feel, the wife gets angry at her husband. She punishes her husband by not speaking to him. She pouts and makes her husband's life miserable. The husband had no intention of hurting his wife. He loves his wife and appreciates her every single day. He doesn't believe he should be obligated to express his love for his wife on a single day. Had he known how important their anniversary was to his wife, the husband would have made a point of remembering it. Rather than have a mature conversation about this, through which they both reach a deeper mutual understanding of each other's needs, the husband's respect for his wife diminishes. The wife acts like a child and does not give her husband the opportunity to do things differently next time. She does not allow him to understand her needs.

Eventually, the wife stops pouting. Maybe she and her husband have the conversation they should have had in the first place. Next time their anniversary rolls around, the husband does something special for his wife out of obligation, so that he doesn't incur her wrath. He doesn't act out of a genuine desire to make his wife happy. His actions are contrived to protect him, as opposed to acting with the sincere desire to express love for his wife.

The failure to communicate or communicating in an immature way breeds resentment. When every time your partner does something to upset you, you pout or say, "I'm fine," you do not give your partner the opportunity to behave differently the next time. Part of the courtship process is learning your partner's likes and dislikes and teaching your partner yours. By refusing to have mature, calm, and respectful conversations about your likes and dislikes, pet-peeves (no matter how silly you may perceive them to be), quirks, and sensitivities, your partner will continue to repeat certain behaviors. Each time he or she does, you will grow more resentful, as the behavior is hurtful or annoying to you. Of course, your partner does not have the benefit of knowing this. After all, you told him or her you're "fine." In turn, your partner will also grow more resentful. Your partner may feel like nothing he or she does makes you happy—that you are always upset. Something that could have easily been resolved with a simple conversation between two adults turns into the very thing that leads to mutual resentment and the demise of the relationship.

You and your partner become two bottles of soda water, repeatedly and vigorously shaken until the pressure forces the cap to explode. And this would have been totally avertible had each of you spoken up.

Communication is not solely limited to speaking. It requires you and your partner to also *listen* to and *hear* one another. Listening means you hear what your partner says. Hearing means you modify or adjust your behavior in response to what your partner says. If after you share your feelings with your partner, your partner continues to behave in the same exact way, then your partner does not *hear* you.

For example, one partner, let's call him Jeff, always leaves his dirty dishes in the sink after dinner. Jeff's partner, let's call her Susan, begrudgingly cleans Jeff's dishes each night. She wishes that Jeff would clean up after himself. Susan feels that by leaving the dishes in the sink, Jeff expects her to clean up after him. She feels like she is Jeff's maid. Susan calmly and nicely expresses her frustration to Jeff and asks that he make an effort to clean his own dishes. Jeff nods his head and agrees. The next night, after dinner, Jeff places his dirty plate and fork in the sink. Susan cleans Jeff's plate and hopes that tomorrow night, Jeff will clean up after himself. The next night, Jeff, again, leaves his dirty dishes in the sink after dinner.

Susan communicated her feelings to Jeff. Jeff did *listen* to Susan. When Susan asked that he clean his dishes, Jeff nodded his head and agreed, signaling to Susan that he acknowledged her words. But Jeff didn't *hear* Susan. This seemingly trivial act of leaving his dishes in the sink made Susan feel belittled and disrespected. The dishes were a symptom of a larger issue—that Jeff felt it was Susan's job to clean his messes. Jeff's failure to adjust his behavior even after Susan expressed her feelings to him has greater implications to the relationship. Jeff's behavior sends the message to Susan that her feelings are not important to him. Jeff's conduct conveys to Susan that he is unwilling to inconvenience himself in the slightest for her. Consequently, Susan will grow to resent Jeff. Going forward in the relationship, she will refrain from sharing her feelings with Jeff, as she knows Jeff does not care enough about her to make even the most minor modification to his behavior. Every unexpressed frustration will gnaw at Susan until she can't stand Jeff. The very sight of him triggers her.

By not listening to, or rather, not hearing Susan, Jeff discourages future communication. Communication requires not only the act of expression, but the acts of listening and hearing. Communication is akin to the wood beams and nails that make up the frame of a house. Each time we communicate a feeling, need, or want to our partner and our partner adjusts his or her behavior to accommodate that feeling, need, or want, another support beam is secured into place. Communication deepens each partner's understanding of the other's needs. *Both* partners must participate in the communication dance to strengthen the foundation of the relationship.

Teamwork

Marriage is a partnership. Often, a client will come to my office and say something along the lines of: "We don't have any assets. The house is in my name. My bank accounts and 401(k) are in my name. We kept everything separate." At least in the State of California, with limited exceptions, everything you earn during marriage—regardless of who earns it—is what is called "community property." This means 50 percent of that property is yours and 50 percent of that property is your spouse's. Again, with rare exception, when a property is purchased during a marriage, even when the title to that property is held in one person's name, the property is presumed to be community property.

More often than not a housewife will come to my office believing her husband is entitled to 100 percent of the couple's assets. By that same token, her husband also believes that his wife is entitled to nothing because *he* is the one who worked and physically earned all of the income during the marriage. California is one of a mere number of states in the United States that is what is called a "community property state." Although community property states are in the country's minority, the respective legislative bodies in these community property states recognize something fundamental about successful relationships. Whether he or she stays home to raise the children or whether he or she goes to work to earn an income for the household, each partner contributes to the marriage. In his or her own way, each partner advances the team. So, when I see that during their marriage, two people maintained entirely separate bank accounts or they split the bill when they went out to restaurants, the reason their marriage failed is fairly obvious to me. They never viewed themselves as teammates playing for the same team. Rather, they perceived themselves as individuals playing for different teams. Before you get defensive, not all couples who keep their assets separate are destined for divorce. I do not deal in relationships that work. I deal in relationships that do not. I am certain that many couples that keep their assets separate have successful relationships. Keeping assets separate is not so much the problem as it is the symptom of a larger problem.

Usually, partners keep their assets separate because they do not perceive themselves to be a unit. Maintaining separate bank accounts does not automatically mean a couple is incapable of working together as a team. It does suggest that the couple does not understand themselves to play for the *same* team.

I happen to be a hockey fan, so I will use a hockey analogy. In hockey, when a player scores a goal, the announcer not only acknowledges the name of the player who scored the goal, he *also* acknowledges the name of the teammate who assisted the player who scored the goal. Hockey understands that the player never could have scored a goal unless one of his teammates passed the puck to him. Consequently, the player who made the goal and the player who assisted him get recognition for the scored goal.

A relationship is no different. A wife gets a promotion. The team wins. High-five. A husband gets a raise. The team wins. High-five. You and your partner are driving on a long stretch of highway in the middle of nowhere. You get a flat tire. One of you searches online for instructions on how to change a tire and talks the other through the steps. The stronger of you helps tighten the lug nuts after the spare is on. After a thirty-minute delay, you and your partner drive off, but not before you high-five one another for working together to find a solution to your *shared* problem. You get the picture. (In case it wasn't obvious—I happen to be quite fond of high-fives. That is what winning teams do to celebrate their victories.)

In a marriage, both partners are furthering common, or *shared* goals. This is another reason (among many) that, from the inception of your relationship, you must establish that you and your partner share fundamental life values.

Let me be explicitly clear: your relationship does not stop you from setting and accomplishing goals independently. A successful relationship requires each partner to support the other in the pursuit of his or her individual goals. In a relationship, you and your partner additionally set *team* goals.

Perhaps you and your partner wish to purchase a home. It will take the efforts of both partners to earn an income and save up for the down payment. Maybe you and your partner hope to start a family. When your first child is born, you and your partner will need to work together, sharing the responsibility for those nighttime feeds and changing diapers. Throughout your child's life, you will need to make important decisions *together*. Your inability to do so can and likely will detrimentally impact your child's well-being. At the crux of many acrimonious divorce battles is two people fighting over medical and educational decisions that both parents must jointly make on their child's behalf. Ironically, the parents are getting divorced *because* they cannot agree. They fundamentally value different things. This is an obvious recipe for disaster.

You and your partner have decided to have children. You discussed this prior to marriage. Great! You both agreed that, ideally, you want two children. Excellent! You even decided your children would be raised in the Catholic faith, as you have identified that this is what you both *fundamentally* value. Wonderful! But how good are you and your partner at passing the proverbial puck to one another?

When you disagree, do you respectfully communicate to resolve conflicts, or does your partner stop speaking to you until you apologize? Does your partner acknowledge when he or she is wrong? Are you able to recognize and admit when you are wrong? *You see, a solid relationship is not characterized by its good times, but by how well you and your partner work together to resolve personal disagreements and life challenges.* Sometimes, the problems may not be between you and your partner. Often, these problems may be external. In the face of adversity, do you and your partner work together, or do you allow challenges to drive you apart? Do you successfully handle conflicts in a way that strengthens your bond and deepens your mutual respect?

If, during your courtship, you and your partner do not successfully work as a team, then how do you expect to do so when life demands it of you? And life *will* demand it of you! If you cannot work together to change a tire, how do you expect to work together to raise a child? First time parents are often surprised by how difficult it actually is. Having a child is a deeply humbling reality check. After having a child of my own, I now understand why so many marriages fail after a child is introduced into the relationship dynamic. Parenthood carries such enormous responsibilities that parents are asked to take on while simultaneously struggling with paralyzing sleep deprivation, postpartum hormonal shifts, and a general sense of exasperation. For this very reason, dating and courtship must be used to ascertain true compatibility. Sure, having fun together at a music festival when you're twenty-five is an important part of the relationship—but it isn't the part that is going to sustain the relationship over time or ensure its longevity.

You yearn to start a family. Years go by and you are unable to conceive. After a barrage of tests, you establish that your partner is infertile. Do you work together to achieve a solution, or do you point fingers and blame your partner for shattering your dreams? Do you support each other through multiple grueling and costly rounds of IVF treatments? Do you encourage each other through years of rejection as you wait to adopt? Do you hold a grudge against your partner when you finally decide to go through life childless? Does your partner sabotage the relationship to cope with his or her guilt? Life does not always go according to plan. Is your partner one with whom you can chart life's many unknowns? The last two lines of Percy Bysshe Shelley's poem "Mutability" read: "Man's yesterday may ne'er be like his morrow;/

Naught may endure but Mutability." Shelley so poignantly reminds us that the only certainty in life is how very uncertain it is. Make no mistake: life *will* be uncertain. Yes, you both had an awesome time riding your bicycles in the nude at Burning Man. This provides absolutely no insight into how well you will work together to resolve unforeseeable obstacles. Life is not the Playa, and in the real world, there are laws against indecent exposure.

Take, for instance, if your three-year-old is diagnosed with autism. He throws tantrums in public, has difficulty socializing with other children at school, and he does not listen to you or your partner at home. It could be that your partner refuses to accept the diagnosis. It could be that you have extremely different ideas on how to help your child. You are determined to use every available resource to get your child to a high-functioning level. Suddenly, you recall that one time you and your partner were driving through Italy and your rental car ran out of gas. You immediately started looking for solutions. The cost be damned, you turned on your data roaming to locate the nearest town or gas station. Rather than get out his phone, turn on his data roaming, and start looking for a taxi or ride-sharing service that could drive you into town or take you somewhere you could purchase gas to bring back to your car, your partner took this opportunity to lecture you about how irresponsible you are and to reprimand you for not refueling at the last gas station.

Sure, your partner has every right to be upset. But this isn't the time or place for finger-pointing. Yes, you should have filled up at the last gas station. Maybe you thought, "Hey, I still have half a tank. There is bound to be another gas station before I actually need to refill." What good does it do to reprimand you when the moment demands you work together to find a solution to your *shared* dilemma? Your partner is right, so you justify his or her behavior—and in the process, you overlook its greater implications. If this were a job interview, such unwarranted hysterics would automatically disqualify you. The interviewer would say: "I'm sorry. I don't think you are quite what we are looking for." Yet, when it comes to selecting someone for the position of life-mate, we put up with unacceptable behaviors. When you ran out of gas in Italy, your partner turned against you rather than working with you. This should have been an indication that maybe your partner is not a team player. He or she will not make a good teammate in life. You get married anyway. Good idea?

Now, fast forward to you, your partner, and your autistic child. The very person who berated you for letting the gas tank run empty is the same person with whom you must make decisions for your special needs child. This person believes your child will outgrow his or her behavioral issues. You strenuously disagree. Your partner is unwilling to get the necessary help for your child. In turn, your child's behavioral issues worsen due to your inability to work together as a team to do what is best for him or her. Your child suffers. For there to be any progress, you and your partner must jointly and consistently implement the recommendations of your child's occupational therapist, behaviorist, and pediatrician. Or, together, you must search for some alternative modality of treatment on which you both agree. Instead, you and your partner grow to resent one another.

Eventually, you decide to end your marriage—something I could have predicted after that whole Italian gas fiasco. You will wage a financially and emotionally costly battle over who gets to make major decisions concerning your child's health, education, and welfare. You most definitely do not trust your partner to make such decisions. After all, your partner is unwilling to so much as admit your child has autism. Conversely, your partner believes you are projecting your neuroses onto your child and that you are unnecessarily burdening your child with behavioral and occupational therapy, supplements, and visits to various specialists. Since your positions are so diametrically opposed, nothing will get accomplished when the judge orders you and your partner to jointly make decisions for your child. Your child will suffer as a direct consequence of you and your partner's inability to work as a team. If only you had not been so dismissive of your partner's reaction that one time you ran out of gas because, I mean, come on, who else would be down to walk around naked at Burning Man with you? It seems almost laughable when put this way, right? But most people don't view their relationships with this level of honest, objective scrutiny.

Nobody expects his or her child to be ill. It happens, though. In the United States, one in fifteen children suffer from multiple chronic conditions. I don't say this to scare you; the statistics are pretty daunting. You should expect the best but prepare for the worst. The future is unknown. You must be sure you and your partner are equipped to work together to effectively problem solve. *While you cannot be certain of your future, you should be certain that you and your partner can work together through any future.*

Long ago, I represented a woman whose child was afflicted with cystic fibrosis. My client and her husband both wanted children. They never expected their child would be born with a fatal illness. As I came to learn, cystic fibrosis is a progressive, degenerative disease where the mucus in the lungs and other organs clogs the airways and traps bacteria, leading to infections, extensive lung damage, and eventually lung failure. It's really, really awful. My client had devoted her existence to improving the quality of her child's life and maximizing her child's life expectancy. As part of her daily routine, the child was to use nebulizers and various machines, which would deliver medication to the lungs. Each parent was to have and use this apparatus when the child was in his or her custody. Often, the dad failed to use this equipment, swearing that his child's condition was not as "bad" as my client made it out to be. It was based on the dad's seeming denial of the child's condition that my client sought sole legal and physical custody. My client wanted the right to make all major decisions concerning the child's health, and she wanted the child in her exclusive custody so that my client could ensure the child received consistent treatment.

I won't psychoanalyze the dad or deviate too far from my point. But it seemed the dad was diminishing the severity of his child's condition to assuage his own feelings of guilt. As the parent of this child, the dad could not help but think that his genetics were responsible for the child's illness. He brought this child into a world where her life was filled with suffering. By denying the severity of his child's illness, the dad managed to both assuage the guilt he felt for bringing this child into the world and convince himself that this terrible disease would not eventually take his child from him. He thought, "If my child is not that sick, then, my child will survive."

Unfortunately, this scenario is quite prevalent. Although the severity of the disease varies, I watch so many parents downplay or altogether deny that their child struggles with chronic conditions, crippling mental illness, or severe behavioral issues. Such scenarios underscore the reasons teamwork is crucial to a relationship. In this case of the child with cystic fibrosis, if the dad had worked together with my client to seek out every available remedy and treatment for their daughter, then he could have prolonged his child's life, or at least provided her with a better standard of living. Instead, the child was acutely aware that her parents were involved in an acrimonious custody battle, of which—at least in this child's mind—she was the cause. Despite the fact that my client and the dad were fighting to do what each of them thought best for their child, that fight came at their child's expense. The stress exacerbated the child's condition. And, as this child was truly ill and required the course of treatment my client insisted upon, the dad's failure to provide this treatment during his custodial time likely wors-ened the child's condition.

The job interview does not end on your first date. It continues up until you decide to get married. It *is* the reason you decide to get married . . . or not. Dating must be approached critically. Overlooking and dismissing the clues will not obviate the problems. A blind person may not see a car driving toward him or her. This does not mean that the car is not there. We all know that sweeping dust under the rug hides the dust. The only way to get rid of the dust is to dispose of it. Working together as a team may prove less important during the courtship phase of your relationship. Hopefully, your life is long. There is no denying that your life to date has been replete with obstacles, all of which you have successfully overcome *on your own*. When you are in a relationship, those problems are no longer your own. They are no longer yours, alone, to overcome. They are the team's problems, and the team must possess the tools to, together, conquer any obstacles.

When you and your partner are unable to work together to change that tire or locate the nearest gas station, your relationship will not sur-vive the challenges life will invariably hurl at you. More importantly, you will suffer, your partner will suffer, and your future children will suffer. I know this sounds bleak. Reality can be bleak. By not playing for the same team, you play for opposing teams. Opposing teams battle one another for victory. Inevitably, one team will win. The other will lose. You and your partner *both* win only when you play for the *same* team. Otherwise, *I* win.

Respect

We can't talk about respect without first defining it. A number of sources define "respect" differently. However, every source's definition includes the word "admiration," and suggests that such admiration is given to another for this individual's "achievements" or "qualities." It follows that a person to whom we give our respect has achieved something we admire. He or she possesses qualities we value. We give our admiration to someone *because* of his or her achievements and qualities.

By selecting a partner whose qualities we don't particularly value or whose achievements we don't really appreciate, we are settling. When so many people settle on their choice of life partner, it is no wonder so many relationships fail. Settling is choosing the comfortable option rather than the *best* option. Often, settling means selecting an option even when we know a better option exists. In the chapter "Have No Fear, Your Intelligence Is Here," we addressed the myriad of reasons people settle. By its very definition, settling is the antithesis of admiration. You are not with this person because you truly admire his or her amazing qualities. You are with this person out of convenience, dysfunction, or fear. When you settle, your relationship is devoid of the last, albeit equally important, Pillar—Respect.

Why is it so important to respect your partner—to admire his or her achievements or qualities? The person with whom you choose to share the rest of your life should be a person who brings out the best in you; who makes you the best version of yourself. You should be with someone you look up to, not someone who disappoints you. When your partner possesses qualities you revere, you admire him or her. You feel proud to share your life with such an amazing and wonderful person. Perhaps this person pushes you to grow in ways you never imagined. And, when your partner possesses qualities you admire and look up to, it suggests you believe you are good enough and deserving of a partner who possesses these inspirational qualities. In stark contrast, when you settle, you feel you do not deserve to be with someone whose qualities you admire. You feel that someone who possesses qualities you admire is too good for you. What do the next fifty years of your life look like if you spend them with someone you don't admire versus someone you do?

Let's look at an example. You settled. You and your partner eventually have a child. Your child is the age at which he or she is ready to attend preschool. You and your partner have done extensive research on the top preschools in the area. You both love your child and want the very best for him or her. You just happen to disagree on what is best. You want your child to attend a prestigious preschool from which children matriculate to the top private schools in your city and, ultimately, go on to attend Ivy League universities. You believe it is never too early to start thinking about college. Your partner wants your child to just enjoy childhood. Your partner thinks your child should enroll in a neighborhood preschool attended by an ethnically diverse group of children—a preschool where there is little structure. Your partner thinks preschool children should not have to worry about college. Neither of you is right. Neither of you is wrong. You and your partner simply have different ideas on what is right for your child. You do not particularly admire any of your partner's qualities. You had been dating for six years before you got married and, while neither one of you was eager to commit to the other at any point prior to that time, your options were to either get married or break up, so you opted for the former. It was convenient. Besides, deciding who got to keep the stemless wine glasses seemed too unpleasant an undertaking.

As you do not really admire any of your partner's qualities all that much, you do not particularly respect your partner's opinion. You are not necessarily open to discussing which school would be better for your child. Ultimately, you do not respect your partner's beliefs and you don't think him or her all that intelligent. How dare he or she sabotage your child's chances of getting into Harvard or Yale! This becomes a fight. Perhaps you demand your child attend the school you chose.

Your partner gives in. He or she doesn't want to fight about it. He or she is upset, though. Your partner doesn't feel such a young child should be subjected to so much structure and rigidity. Maybe your partner opposes your choice so strenuously that you and your partner decide to delay the conversation until the following year. Your child is young. He or she can start preschool next year. Or maybe you compromise on a third option with which neither of you is happy, leaving you resenting one another as you *both* believe your child is attending a sub-par school. If your idiot partner would have just agreed to your child attending the school *you* wanted, your child would be at a good preschool. You think to yourself, "Great, now my child's life is ruined."

Respect means you and your partner communicate and share ideas and opinions with one another. It means that when your partner tells you something with which you disagree, you consider it. Can you and your partner have a conversation about politics or debate other heated subjects without looking down on each other's viewpoints and losing respect for one another? (The answer is yes!) You admire your partner, and consequently, you value your partner's beliefs and thoughts. Respect and communication are symbiotic. You and your partner communicate effectively because you appreciate your partner's input, even when you disagree with it. Without respect, communication is impossible. When the Respect Pillar topples, the Communication Pillar crumbles alongside it, threatening the stability of your relationship structure.

Chapter 11:
Children: The Marriage Truth Serum

"Hide nothing, for time, which hears all
and sees all, exposes all."
—Sophocles

C ongratulations! You've chosen the perfect shade of celadon green for your jungle-themed nursery. You bought every baby gizmo and gadget available on the market (and even some that aren't). Your best friend threw you the most beautiful baby shower, leaving everyone on social media beyond envious of you. You planned a fairy-tale gender reveal party, befitting a top influencer. I guess the only thing left to do now is live happily ever after, right? Nope. Wrong.

At the end of the chapter "What in the 'F-Word' Is a Fundamental Value?" I (perhaps annoyingly) belabored the notion that one cannot build a foundation with a person with whom he or she does not share fundamental values. While the reasons for this are plentiful, none serves as greater proof than having children. No, not every couple will have children. For the majority that do, a child will shine an inescapable, blinding spotlight on any cracks in the relationship, leaving a giant chasm in its wake.

In defining fundamental values, we ascertained that our fundamental values characterize our identity, our moral compass, and our outlook on life. We determined that these principles or standards shape the decisions we make in our lives. It follows that a person who shares similar principles or standards will make decisions in a similar way. We seek this in a partner not because we are superior or because our way is best, but because marriage demands that we work together as a team. When we and our partner do not navigate obstacles in a similar and like-minded manner, we clash. Decisions don't get made. We end up at odds with one another.

In every contentious divorce, litigation is often inevitable when two people cannot agree on child custody and visitation issues. One or both of them will not agree on the manner in which property should be divided or the debt should be allocated. Of course they can't agree! If they could agree, then they wouldn't be getting divorced. And, if they shared fundamental values, they would most likely agree on most of the issues they end up fighting about during their divorce.

Having a child bestows upon you and your partner the responsibility to jointly make decisions for a human life that is entirely helpless and dependent on the two of you. You will need to make decisions together. By failing to make decisions in a similar way, you and your partner will find yourselves clashing with one another. This will result in frequent heated arguments. Those arguments will seem all the more personal and hurtful when you feel you are being criticized for your parenting. You know you are making the best decision. Your partner's belief that your decision is wrong or bad will feel like he or she is driving a dagger through your heart. When it comes to your child, you perceive every challenge to your judgment as an utter betrayal, carrying with it a palpable sting like no other you have ever experienced.

Two people with dissonant beliefs or values having children will be incapable of co-parenting and, consequently, at odds with one another. In the most obvious example—religion—a person who staunchly insists upon raising his or her child in a particular faith cannot successfully co-parent with a person who unwaveringly insists upon raising his or her child in another faith. Both parents want what is best for their child. They simply define "best" differently. When one parent gets his or her way, the other will feel he or she is not doing what is best for the child. He or she is left with two choices—to go to war with his or her partner over the issue, or to give in and internalize the resentment. And the thing about resentment is that it always boils over. Repressing emotions for an extended period of time is impossible. Resentment is too powerful and all-consuming an emotion.

Therefore, it should come as little surprise that the majority of cases I encounter involve children. I know exactly what you're thinking: these couples did not share fundamental values to begin with. So, why didn't they break up sooner? Why did it take having children to destroy a relationship between two people lacking in fundamental values? (That's what you were thinking, right?) Sure, children are exhausting succubae, who drain every last ounce of life from our souls like adorable energy vampires. I'm kidding, of course. All jokes aside, though, children are not the problem. A child is not tantamount to a marriage death sentence. Believe it or not, a child can actually enhance a strong relationship. However, when a couple does not share fundamental values, a child is a veritable grim reaper, brandishing its formidable scythe.

When I first started practicing Family Law, I recall being surprised by the fact that most marriages ended after ten to thirteen years, among couples having mostly two to three children. At twenty-six years old, I naively thought it must be some sort of strange coincidence. I thought there must be some truth to that "seven-year itch" curse. "Another thirteen-year marriage with two kids?" I wondered. Over the years, I gained experience and insight into the reason so many couples with children ended their marriages after roughly a decade.

Yes, children do demand our attention, often leaving us too tired to function. They are a leviathan responsibility taking precedence over all else. They may, and frequently do, inhibit our ability to be spontaneous. They detract our attention from our partner. Yet, unless you have completely and irrationally romanticized parenting, you already knew it was going to be a monumental commitment. It's no secret. Babies wake up every several hours. You will spend months on end deprived of sleep. Just when you get used to sleeping again, they hit a sleep regression and you are, again, woken multiple times per night, every single night. You should not be shocked by the fact that you will miss out on fun events and plans when you don't have childcare. You know you will be relegated to the playground, chasing after a toddler with hawk-like precision, ensuring they don't catapult face-first into a pole. All you really want to do is sit on the couch and binge watch anything or mindlessly scroll through your phone. (I speak from experience.) You will often be left far too exhausted to be intimate with your partner.

After giving birth, and even in the years that follow, women may feel less attractive. Consequently, they might perceive themselves as less desirable. A woman may project her insecurities on to her partner. Though it is likely untrue, she assumes her partner is no longer physically attracted to her. This causes her to feel even worse about herself, promulgating a self-perpetuating cycle of self-doubt and sadness that will take an inevitable toll on the relationship. With her partner's support, this woman may eventually regain her self-confidence. In the process of supporting a woman postpartum, her partner may feel hopeless and helpless. In short, when you have a baby, it's no longer all acid trips at music festivals and backpacking through Europe with impunity. Shit gets real.

Babies, toddlers, and teenagers are not angelic dolls who simply fit into your prepackaged life. When you don't have children, all of this is intangible and near impossible to fathom. From an intellectual perspective, though, you can conceptually understand it.

While the reasons that lead to the demise of a relationship have no legal significance to the litigation of a Family Law case (at least not in California), they are nevertheless inextricable to it. Family Law is so emotionally charged that virtually each potential client begins his or her initial consultation with me by sharing the intimate details of the relationship and the events that precipitated its downfall. Of course, each client and every relationship are unique. But the patterns are so redundant. Clients are often shocked when I describe their soon-to-be-ex-spouse—whom I never met—with such uncanny particularity. I often hear, "How did you know?" "It's like you've met him/her." I'm actually starting to question whether I possess psychic abilities. (I'm kidding again.) I relentlessly watch people enter relationships for the same wrong reasons. Then, I watch those relationships fail for the same predictable reasons. The dysfunctional dynamics are textbook—Relationsh*ts 101. Sometimes, I feel like that parent who warns her child not to run with sharp scissors. When the child inevitably falls and gets hurt, I roll my eyes, sigh deeply and admonish, "I told you so." Except, in my line of work, I meet the child after the fall. The point of this book is to get to the child *before* the fall.

So, you're on a second or third date. The chemistry oozes. You're ready to rip your clothes off. You're definitely not thinking about your future children. That would be crazy—nay, deem you certifiable, right? No, let's not get ahead of ourselves. As you now know, you should be using each date as an opportunity to ascertain whether you and your date (the would-be mother or father of your child) share fundamental values. When shit gets real, will this relationship survive? Those fundamental values will prove critical when raising a child together. To put it bluntly, without shared fundamental values, you cannot co-parent. Period.

Eckhart Tolle said, "To love is to recognize yourself in another." Before you make the very serious decision to have a child with someone, you must be absolutely certain that you value the same things in life, and in turn will strive to raise your child in the same way. Having a child carries with it new and uncharted challenges. Your relationship will likely survive an argument over whether you and your partner should travel to Cabo or Rome for your summer getaway. Momentous decisions—such as whether or not to vaccinate a child or whether to raise a child in the city where one partner's family lives versus raising that child in the city where the other partner's family lives—result in far more insurmountable conflict. You know that, without shared fundamental values, you cannot build a solid foundation. It therefore stands to reason that if you and your partner do not share fundamental values, the foundation of your relationship will also be weak. A child is the inescapable relationship truth serum, administered to each respective foundational Pillar, exposing its weakness.

A child equals sudden death to a relationship lacking in fundamental values and a solid foundation. I will share several scenarios that I see frequently in my practice, which poignantly illustrate the ways children destroy weak marriages:

Control/Trust Issues

Far too often, I watch one parent—most frequently, the mother—feel the need to control, micromanage, and even dictate every aspect of the child's life, marginalizing the other parent's opinions and involvement. As a mother, I am keenly familiar with the maternal drive to protect one's child. Intangible forces inexplicably possess me to do anything and everything I think absolutely best for my son. On a primal level, mothers are hardwired to nurture and shield their children. These maternal instincts serve an evolutionary purpose, rendering them virtually uncontrollable. We don't really think about it. It is as though we are robots, powered by external controls, fulfilling our biologically programmed function. This is not to say fathers lack these instincts. I merely suggest that, in my practice, such tendencies seem to be more prevalent among mothers. And, without question, there is an undeniable scientific reason for it.

In Family Law, we typically refer to the parent who takes it upon himself or herself to make the decisions for the child or to dictate the other parent's level of involvement as the "gatekeeper" parent. The relationship usually plays out something like this: one parent—in this example, the mom—cooks all meals for the child, bathes the child, unilaterally determines which extracurricular activities the child will be enrolled in, selects the child's doctor, dentist, and other healthcare providers, takes the child to doctor's appointments, arranges playdates, and takes the child to social activities. She does not consult the father in the decision-making process, but informs him only after the fact, if at all. For whatever reason (which should have been telling when they were dating), the mother does not deem the father capable of making decisions—at least not ones that meet her standards. The father goes along with the mother's decisions. Over time, the father retreats altogether from the decision-making process. He wants to participate in the decision-making. He doesn't need to. He knows mother will make good decisions. He also knows the mother will reject any opinions that deviate from her edicts.

Ultimately, the father grows to feel inadequate. In his mind, he loves his child and is perfectly adept at making decisions for him or her. In anointing herself the oligarch of decision-making, the mother implicitly declares the father incapable. In one fell swoop, the mother reaps destruction on the relationship, delivering a powerful roundhouse-kick to the Trust, Teamwork, Communication, and Respect Pillars. In case your math skills are as awful as mine, that's four of the Five Pillars!

Interestingly, this dynamic seems to most frequently play out when a child is diagnosed with autism spectrum disorder (ASD). The ubiquitous mother in this scenario, let's call her Sandra, takes it upon herself to make appointments with various specialists to first obtain a diagnosis. Once the child is diagnosed, Sandra performs endless research to secure all available resources and therapeutic modalities to maximize the child's success. Sandra does not involve the father when making decisions. In this scenario, let's call the ubiquitous father James. Sandra may notify James of her choices. She does not ask James's opinion. Suspecting the child's behavioral issues may be attributable more to the discord in their home than to an actual medical condition, James might disagree with the diagnosis. This, of course, further infuriates Sandra and disincentivizes her from seeking James's opinion—driving a deeper wedge in their relationship. Sandra concludes that James does not care about their child. She comes to feel isolated and resentful. Although James may not entirely agree with the diagnosis, he doesn't see any harm in pursuing the therapies. He goes along with Sandra's choices. Even if James fully agrees with the ASD diagnosis, he entirely removes himself from the decision-making process. He knows Sandra will obtain the best therapeutic modalities available for their child. He trusts Sandra will handle it. Besides, nothing James does or says is good enough anyway.

In some ways, Sandra grows to derive personal validation from her child's diagnosis. With every new therapy she obtains for her child, she reaffirms for herself, "I am a great mother." In her mind, she cares more about the child than James does, and therefore, she convinces herself she is the superior parent. This makes her feel better about herself, while also reinforcing and even justifying her thoughts about James. In Sandra's mind, the more she does, the worse James is. In essence, her tautological thinking results in a self-fulfilling outcome.

Sandra does not allow James to make any decisions, so James refrains from making them. Sandra is then upset with James for not making any decisions. It's indeed apparent that Sandra has placed James in an unwinnable position.

James is not without fault, though. Instead of communicating his feelings to Sandra and engaging in a meaningful conversation with her, he withdraws. Had James been more assertive and established boundaries, Sandra would not have succeeded in marginalizing him. Had Sandra expressed the way she truly felt, instead of expecting James to guess, James might have adjusted his behavior accordingly. (Sandra wanted James to "want to wash the dishes.") Perhaps they might have avoided divorce. You do not wait until you are married to work on your communication skills. You must first establish that you and your partner communicate effectively *before* committing to marriage. Those rings on your fingers are not magical. You don't live in Middle Earth. The act of slipping rings on each other's fingers will not resuscitate a faulty Pillar. Even the most spectacular diamond eternity band cannot miraculously mend the cracks in your relationship.

Let's take a closer look at this scenario in the context of the foundational Pillars—the first of which is Trust. If Sandra trusted James, she would have trusted him to make sound decisions on behalf of their child. But she does not allow him to make decisions, as she believes she will make better decisions. Maybe she thinks he'll make downright awful decisions. Yes, a mother's need to protect her child is primordial. But a mother should not feel she needs to protect her child from its own father. The fact that Sandra is compelled to protect her child from James signifies a lack of trust, which most likely predated the birth of their child. Sandra always knew she did not trust James to make important life decisions. Whether she admitted this to herself is a different issue.

Perhaps, during their courtship, Sandra unconsciously assumed control or micromanaged everything from travel arrangements to dinner reservations, social engagements, James's health, and paying the bills each month. Sandra did not take the time to scrutinize her behavior. She simply concluded that James was incapable of taking the initiative. Had Sandra possessed any insight into her conduct, she would have understood that she did not trust James to take care of himself, let alone their future offspring. This would have and should have provided Sandra with an invaluable clue. She just wasn't thinking about her unborn children at the time.

It might be that James wasn't fully capable of taking charge. Maybe Sandra struggled with trust issues. Maybe she was just a control freak. Or James felt comfortable taking the back seat, entrusting Sandra to make the decisions. Possibly, James truly lacked initiative. Regardless of whether Sandra was controlling, or James was unassertive, the couple's issues speak to an inability to work together as a team. Each time Sandra took charge, she sent a resounding message to James that she didn't trust him—she didn't deem him capable. James heard her loud and clear.

Sandra should have reflected on her behavior. Did she struggle with trust and control issues? Did she genuinely perceive James as incapable of taking the initiative? Had James stopped to evaluate the situation, he might have realized that Sandra didn't trust him. He would have understood that this made him feel inadequate, even resentful. These issues should have been identified and addressed by *both* Sandra *and* James prior to committing their lives to one another, and most certainly before they decided to have a child together. Sandra and James (like so many others) lacked the requisite insight—ultimately sentencing their relationship to failure.

Did Sandra and James bury their heads in the sand to avoid an inevitable outcome or were they completely oblivious? Was getting married and having children more important to each of them than marrying and having children with the right person? It could have been a little bit of all the above. This scenario, albeit prevalent, is specific to these two individuals—Sandra and James. Yet, in a broader sense, Sandra and James exemplify something true of most failed relationships. The demise of a relationship is almost assured when two people overlook the inequity in their power dynamic, which brings us to our next Pillar, Trust. Let Sandra and James (along with my long roster of other clients) serve as a sobering didactic. If you do not trust your partner to make decisions, how do you expect to make decisions with your partner?

Trust between two people is rudimentary to the co-parenting relationship. Often when we think of trust in relationships, we think of infidelity. But trust is so much bigger. Trust is not just a function of whether you believe your partner will or will not cheat on you. Trust requires you to have faith in your partner's decisions. When you are dating your partner, ask yourself: "If something happens to me, do I trust this person to make decisions on my behalf when I am incapacitated?" "If we have a child, would I implicitly trust this person to raise this child in my absence?" "Do I believe this person possesses the capacity to make decisions for our child?" "Does this person make good decisions in his or her own life?"

A house with a feeble foundation eventually topples. And a marriage devoid of trust will end in divorce. It doesn't stop there, though. Lack of trust plays itself out in the bitter custody battle. When two parents divorce, with rare exception, they will share custody of their child. This means that neither parent will see their child 100 percent of the time. It also means the child will never spend 100 percent of his or her time with both parents. To me, even in the most amicable divorces, custody is always the most devastating issue. As a parent, I would be utterly destroyed if I did not get to see my child every day. How crushing it must be for a child to see each of his or her parents only several days each week.

A child of divorce can absolutely be happy and well-adjusted. There are many instances where two people successfully co-parent in such a way that their child is relatively unphased. When the divorce is non-contentious, the child can and likely will be very happy. Sadly, this is more the exception than the rule. For the most part, two people who communicate effectively, respect one another, and generally get along, do not get divorced. They get divorced *precisely* because they do not. The lack of respect and inability to communicate often lead to distrust. When one parent does not trust the other, or when one parent feels his or her every behavior is being critiqued by the other, it creates a palpable rift—accompanied by costly and acrimonious litigation, into which the child is inescapably thrust—all due to the fact that Sandra never trusted James and neither she nor James were willing to confront their trust issues during their courtship.

Taken one step further, Sandra's distrust of James emanated from their lack of shared fundamental values. Sandra did not trust James to care for their child, as she and James possessed dissonant views on child-rearing. James was a permissive parent. Sandra was an authoritative parent. They did not fundamentally champion the same beliefs. James knew this well before he and Sandra had children. Sandra shared details about her upbringing with James. She seemed to approve of the way she was raised. The details Sandra shared caused James to raise an eyebrow. But James never spoke up. James also shared details about his upbringing with Sandra. He seemed to approve of the way he was raised. Sandra internally questioned various aspects of James's upbringing. She, too, kept quiet. They agreed they grew up with very different parenting styles, each dismissing his or her concerns about the other's upbringing.

Maybe one day, Sandra and James were enjoying a picnic at the park. A toddler nearby threw a tantrum. Sandra and James both chimed in, judging the parents' handling of the situation. Each commented on the way he or she would have handled it. Their answers were contrasting. They laughed it off. This should have been the part of the job interview that gave each of them pause. Instead, they dismissed what should have been an eye-opening conversation, ignoring the repercussions of doing so. By avoiding their fundamental differences, Sandra and James delayed the inevitable. They didn't realize that their fundamental values would eventually inform their child-rearing. The absence of fundamental values virtually guarantees that when you and your partner become parents, you will be at odds with one another. Obviously, these are not first or second date questions. They *are,* however, questions that need to be answered as the relationship evolves.

A veritable domino effect, when Sandra destroyed the Trust Pillar, she simultaneously knocked down the Teamwork Pillar. You are unlikely to work together with someone you don't trust. Conversely, you are more likely to work with someone you do trust. Teammates are equals. They work alongside one another to make crucial decisions. In the case of Sandra and James, Sandra believed she could win the game without strategizing plays with and passing the ball to her teammate. The more Sandra hogged the ball, the more James questioned his skills as a player, ultimately altogether doubting his abilities. You need not understand the rules of sports to get this analogy. The more James questioned his qualifications, the more Sandra concluded James was incapable of playing the game. James was supposed to be Sandra's teammate. Instead, he sat on the bench, relegated to the sidelines, watching Sandra take control of child rearing and every other aspect of their lives. This left James feeling inadequate in every way. In the Freudian sense, Sandra (figuratively) castrated James.

The psychological and emotional implications of this to the male ego are obvious.

While you are dating—conducting the job interview—you should be deliberately placing yourself in situations to determine whether you and your partner work well as a team. I happen to be a big proponent of international travel to a foreign country where neither you nor your partner speak the language. Of course, not everyone has the means or desire to do this. I highly recommend traveling abroad if it is accessible to you. You and your partner will need to work together to arrange transportation from the airport to your accommodations. The travel will offer invaluable insight into your partner's fundamental values. You will learn whether one of you is an early riser and the other likes to sleep until noon. Is one of you a night owl and the other a morning person? You will determine whether one of you prefers to fastidiously plan an itinerary and the other would rather bumble through the day without any definitive plans. If you are both highly motivated individuals that share the fundamental value of adventure, do you work together when you inevitably get lost, or your car breaks down in an area with no cell service?

However, you need not travel to an exotic destination to determine whether you and your partner work well as a team. Each day, countless situations present themselves that will require you and your partner to pass the proverbial ball to one another. A problem emerges when you bury your heads in the sand rather than use these opportunities to observe and reflect. Most people reach for the broom and sweep these glaring red flags under that notorious rug. They ignore the fact that their partner hogs the ball or doesn't play by the rules of the game. This is easier than ending the relationship.

Yes, breakups are painful. Divorce is excruciating. When children are involved, you are not hurting only yourself, you are dramatically and forever impacting the life of the very child who you—yes, *both* parents—are primally programmed to protect at all costs. When you cannot work together as a team, your relationship will not work— especially once you have a child. Children require day-to-day pivots, adjustments, and compromises, which you cannot make unless you and your partner are able to work cohesively. The momentary pain of a breakup now is far more palatable than lifelong devastation—not just for you, but for the life of the innocent child you bring into this world.

In our example, Sandra can be blamed for bulldozing the Trust and Teamwork Pillars. Yet, as I previously touched upon, Sandra and James are equally to blame for demolishing the third Pillar, Communication. Sandra was always a control freak. Many people are controlling. Not all control freaks end up divorced. James needed to set boundaries. He needed to push back a little when he felt Sandra was controlling him. The more James allowed Sandra to push him, the more she did. Had James pushed back, Sandra would not have succeeded in push-ing James as much as she did. Sandra gravitated toward James, and he to her, because James was passive. He was easy to control, so Sandra controlled him.

Sandra and James were not necessarily wrong for each other, though. Their inability to communicate was the root of their demise. Sandra succeeded in expelling James from the decision-making process. After all, James allowed it. When Sandra began researching resources and therapeutic modalities for their autistic child, James should have par-ticipated. James should have made it known to Sandra that he did not agree with the diagnosis. He could have scheduled a counseling session for him and Sandra to address their differences. He could have arranged an appointment with another specialist to obtain a second opinion. Instead, he retreated and allowed Sandra to take the reins without ever expressing his position. This deepened Sandra's resentment. Mostly,

Sandra probably felt sad that her child's father did not want to do everything possible to help their child succeed in life. That was not necessarily true. She constructed this narrative in her mind, manifesting it into existence. She masked her sadness behind anger. Surely, anger is a stronger and less vulnerable emotion than sadness. Sandra's anger made her feel she was in control. When one feels so completely out of control, he or she will grasp for it at any opportunity. This is human nature. Not surprisingly, Sandra clawed for more and more control.

Or perhaps Sandra and James weren't right for one another to begin with. Had they communicated their true feelings to each other, their relationship might not have deteriorated so bitterly. They might have realized that they both wanted the same thing. Equally possible is the prospect that Sandra and James were genuinely unable to communicate. One or both of them might have lacked the ability to express their feelings to the other. The *reason* for their inability to communicate aside, their failure to communicate came to be the nail in the marriage's coffin.

Sandra and James beautifully illustrate not only the reason communication is so critical to a relationship's survival, but the way the inability to communicate is often symptomatic of something deeper. At this point, we have established that James's inability or unwillingness to voice his opinions encouraged Sandra to take charge and even usurp all of the power in their relationship. Sandra felt James to be incapable of making decisions. She began to lose respect for James and possibly resented him. Why did Sandra seek out a relationship in which she needed to be in control? Why didn't she feel comfortable expressing her true feelings to James? Why did James feel more comfortable retreating than voicing his opinion?

Ostensibly, Sandra and James were unable to communicate with one another because they each brought with them into the relationship certain quirks that were the product of their unaddressed traumas or past experiences. Something in Sandra's life caused her to feel so out of control that the only way to compensate was by micromanaging every detail of her child's and partner's lives. The way Sandra treated James could be the way Sandra's mother treated Sandra's father. Sandra learned that a husband cannot make decisions. It could also be that, as a child, James witnessed his father being denigrated by his mother for asserting an opinion. James learned to keep his mouth shut. James deemed this dynamic perfectly normal, and consequently emulated the power dynamic in his parents' marriage by marrying someone controlling. James also thought that within this power dynamic, a husband must keep his mouth shut or otherwise risk censure from his wife. James did just that. James had no other frame of reference.

Neither Sandra nor James understood the impact that their life experiences had on their communication skills. Ironically, these experiences informed their respective choices in life partner. Sandra and James gravitated toward the familiar, falling into the predictable pitfalls that inevitably accompanied them. Sandra and James could not effectively communicate until they reflected upon the circumstances that led them to choose one another in the first place. Had they done the work prior to starting the relationship, they might not have even been attracted to one another at all. They may have still ended up together. Their relationship might have even succeeded. By recognizing the way their childhood experiences shaped their understanding of relationships, Sandra and James could have learned to communicate more efficaciously. They could have learned to set boundaries for themselves, which, in turn, would have fostered a more equitable power dynamic in their relationship.

Far too often, I watch relationships fail due to the way two people communicate or their outright failure to do so. There is little doubt that the way two people communicate is the direct consequence of their past experiences and traumas. Without gaining an understanding for the ways these experiences or traumas shape our ability or inability to communicate with others, these experiences and traumas will continue to inform our choice of partner. They will go on to dictate our behavior in a relationship.

This book is not a discourse in the ways childhood traumas impact our relationship choices. Nevertheless, I would be remiss if I did not point out how frequently I see my clients' childhood experiences and traumas affect their relationship choices, and then dictate the dynamic of those relationships. This is not to say that participation in therapy is a prerequisite to one's success in a relationship. But if you do feel your parents' dysfunctional relationship was perfectly healthy and normal, then it may be advisable for you to participate in some counseling before beginning a serious relationship. The way you communicate is a function of your past experiences, your childhood, and your upbringing. Any opportunity to reflect upon these things will only help. It certainly can't hurt.

In the case of Sandra and James, Sandra's behavior took a wrecking ball to one final foundational Pillar, Respect. We previously established that respect is given to one whose qualities we admire. Sandra did not admire James's qualities. She abhorred them. She deemed his opinions so worthless that she dubbed herself the parent exclusively qualified to make decisions on their child's behalf. Perhaps Sandra did not believe James made good decisions in his own life, and therefore was incapable of making good decisions for their child.

You need not travel to a foreign country with your partner to glean whether your partner exercises good judgment. You must observe your partner in his or her day-to-day life to determine whether he or she makes life decisions that are admirable to you. When a problem arises in your partner's job, how does he or she handle it? Do you agree with the way he or she handled it? Your partner experiences a conflict with a friend or family member. How does he or she approach it? Do you agree with your partner's approach? Do you feel your partner makes good decisions regarding his or her education, career, living situation, and finances? Do you admire his or her decisions, or do your partner's choices give you pause? Rest assured, when you question your partner's life decisions, you will question your partner's parenting decisions.

Over the years, I have represented a number of female clients who hinted at or altogether dictated to their partners when to propose. In this scenario, the ubiquitous wife, let's call her Mindy, told the ubiquitous husband, let's call him Tom, exactly which ring to purchase and when to pop the question. Tom lacked the initiative to make such decisions on his own. He would not select a ring or propose unless told when and how to do so. Mindy didn't respect Tom. She was so preoccupied with getting married that she did not even realize it. Before Mindy and Tom had children, each of them was clueless to the fact that Mindy's lack of respect for Tom would ultimately destroy the relationship. Mindy was all too happy to have a ring on her finger and a husband to show off to her friends.

Once Mindy and Tom had a child, Mindy assumed complete control over all child-rearing responsibilities. She deemed Tom incapable of taking the initiative to make the meals, bathe their child, or even tuck their child into bed at night. Mindy did not admire Tom. She did not feel he made the best life decisions. He lacked motivation. He was no catch, and quite frankly, Mindy was far too good for Tom. While they were dating, Mindy frequently micromanaged Tom's life. She wanted to improve him. Tom complicitly went along with it. When it was time to parent a child together, Mindy naively wondered why Tom was incapable of taking the initiative. When, on occasion, Tom did take the initiative, Mindy always questioned him. His decisions were never good enough. Mindy did not believe Tom capable of making good decisions. She did not respect him. This isn't a made-up scenario. It is a prevalent one—in fact, so prevalent that it warrants noting. I see Mindys and Toms in my office all the time.

As an outsider reading this scenario, you may think, "Yeah. It's so obvious." Yet, when you are Mindy or Tom, you don't (or don't want to) see the issue. When you are in a relationship, viewing it objectively can be difficult. It can be uncomfortable. Whether your judgment is clouded by infatuation, or whether you don't want to face the inevitable reality of ending your relationship, you ignore the truth. You convince yourself the relationship is right. But what if you approached your own relationship with the same objectivity with which you approach the examples in this book? What if you were to view your own relationship through the lens of an outside observer, recognizing it for what it is, as opposed to what you want it to be? The truth will come out. Burying your head in the sand will not stop whatever is going on above ground.

Parenting is the most unpredictable journey you will ever embark upon. It can place a strain on even the healthiest relationship. Will you and your partner agree on everything? No. Should you? Absolutely not. Making good decisions for your child requires meaningful discussion, predicated on respect for your partner's opinion. You need to trust your partner's judgment and beliefs. You must feel a sense of camaraderie. You are equals. Neither of you needs to act as gatekeeper. You are confident each of you will act in the best interest of your child. This all seems straightforward, right? However, we form relationships and marriages without considering these vital details. Before you decide to bring a child into this world, establish whether you and your partner share the fundamental values necessary to jointly make difficult decisions. Take the time to confirm your relationship is built on a solid foundation. Make the critical inquiry into whether all Five Pillars are sturdy enough to withstand an earthquake of unfathomable magnitude. Children will shake the bedrock of your foundation, testing its fortitude. When the structure of your relationship is not sufficiently sturdy, a child will leave catastrophic devastation in its wake. Retrofit your relationship so that it may withstand any jolt.

Family

I was conflicted whether to discuss family (in the context of having a child) in this section or to include it in the chapter "Meet the Family." Ultimately, I decided to address it in this section for reasons which I hope will become apparent to you.

I am going to offer another example that specifically involves mothers.[1] In this scenario, the mother, let's call her Abigail, was originally from London. She moved to New York for work. She met her partner, let's call him Jonah, while she was living in New York. Abigail and Jonah dated and eventually got married. Jonah was extremely close to his family. His family lived in New York. Jonah's family warmly welcomed Abigail. They even served as somewhat of a surrogate family for Abigail, whose entire family lived in London. Abigail was also close to her family. She found it difficult to live so far away from them. She lived in New York solely to further her career. At her age, she felt the sacrifice was warranted. After several years of dating, Jonah proposed to Abigail. She loved Jonah and wanted to spend her life with him, so

---

1 It may appear as though, by giving examples that involve mothers, I am showing a gender bias. I assure you I am providing you with examples of the most prevalent scenarios I encounter in my practice, in the hope they will serve as a helpful didactic.

she accepted his proposal and decided to create a life with Jonah in New York.

Several years after they were married, Abigail and Jonah had their first child. Jonah's family was very involved. They helped Jonah and Abigail every chance they could. Abigail loved Jonah's parents and appreciated their assistance. Their presence also served as a sad reminder of her parents' absence. When Abigail became a mother, she appreciated her mother in a new way and wanted her mother around to offer advice. She wanted her mother to establish a bond with her child—which was impossible from over three thousand miles away. Abigail began to entertain the idea of returning to London. She knew Jonah would never agree to it, so she bottled up her feelings, growing increasingly depressed. When she could no longer contain her sadness, she broached the subject with Jonah, who immediately rejected the prospect of moving to London—as Abigail knew he would. Abigail was left with two choices: 1) Divorce Jonah and move to London with their child; or 2) Continue to live in New York in misery. She did love Jonah, and she felt she had committed to living in New York when she agreed to marry him. At the same time, their child did not know its maternal grandparents. Abigail began to feel withdrawn from Jonah. She experienced a gamut of emotions, from resentment to regret, from grief to hopelessness.

Eventually, Abigail couldn't take it anymore. She was willing to end the marriage if need be. She wanted to be geographically close to her family. Abigail never planned to live in New York for the rest of her life and had moved there with the thought of living there temporarily until she advanced in her career. One day, she mustered the courage to declare she was moving to London. Jonah loved Abigail and he did not want to live apart from her. And he refused to live so far away from his child. Jonah agreed to move to London. Upon his move, Jonah became depressed. He missed his family, his friends, his job, and his life. Eventually, Abigail and Jonah got divorced.

When you are dating and so deeply in love with your partner, you feel you are willing to make certain sacrifices. You are not thinking about the way these concessions will impact you after you have children. Understanding what it feels like to have children is nearly impossible until you have them. I am asking you to grasp something incomprehensible. You must, though. You and your partner are close to your families. Your families live in different locations. You and your partner will need to be honest with yourselves and with each other. You cannot avoid what will invariably prove to be a difficult conversation—one which may potentially cause you to break up with a person with whom you have an otherwise perfect relationship. Sometimes, no matter how much you love and care for someone, the situation or timing is simply not right. These relationships are perhaps the most difficult to end. The relationship seems right. It is right. *No matter how good a relationship may be, when the circumstances are wrong, the relationship is wrong.* The right person is only right when the circumstances surrounding the relationship are also right. In the case of Abigail and Jonah, the circumstances were not right. Thus, the relationship was wrong.

When you have children, will you be okay living in the city where your partner's family lives and not in the city where your family lives? Is it realistic to travel long distances with a small child? (For those of you who do not have children, I will answer this question for you. It's not.) Do you want your family to be a significant presence in your child's life? Will you be able to live with the fact that they are not? What role do you want your family to play in your child's life, if any? What role does your partner want his or her family to play in your child's life, if any? Do you and your partner plan to have children?

If the answer is "yes," you cannot commit to marriage until each of you answers these questions.

I have litigated many cases in which one parent decides to move to another state or country after the couple has separated. In California, these are called "move away" cases. In crafting orders, the court must decide how often the child travels back and forth for visits. When the child is still too young to travel by himself or herself, who will accompany the child on flights? Who will pay for the child's flights, and who will pay for the accompanying parent's flights? When one parent comes to visit the child in the other city, does he or she stay at a hotel to exercise an extended visit? Does the child stay overnight in the hotel too? Which parent pays for the hotel? Does the child spend an extended period with one parent over school breaks to compensate for the lack of parenting time during the school year? Are you comfortable being away from your child for an entire month while he or she visits the other parent? Are you comfortable seeing your child once a month or once every couple of months after your child has moved to another state or country? Sound complicated? Sound awful? It is.

Yes, you may love your partner. You may have a wonderful relationship. But when you do not wish to live in the same place, divorce—or at the very least, a life filled with misery and resentment—are inevitable.

Boo-hoo. I'm Not Getting Attention.

I'm not sure whether it is biological or societal. For some strange reason, we romanticize babies. I cannot count the number of social media posts I have seen depicting a newborn laying on its mother's chest. Both parents look smitten as they hypnotically gaze at their baby. The caption almost always reads: "My heart is full." Seemingly, people believe that the sentiment encapsulated in this ephemeral, picture-perfect moment represents parenthood. Sorry. (Who am I kidding?

I'm not sorry.) I am, again, the bearer of bad news—your sobering reality check. This single, perfect, and very fleeting moment is not parenthood. Parenthood is messy and imperfect. This is not a book about parenthood, so I will not elaborate on the reasons for that—although, you can likely imagine.

Babies, and more generally, parenthood, can and do take a toll on relationships. The all too pervasive and unrealistic expectations we place on babies and parenthood prove this toll all the more significant. You cannot enter parenthood hoping it will strengthen your bond with your partner. It may. It may also test your relationship. Your relationship will not survive parenthood if it cannot withstand the strain parenthood places on it. Your relationship will survive parenthood only when it is built on a solid foundation and shared fundamental values. When these two F-Words are present in the relationship, parenthood could even strengthen it.

It makes sense, really. So long as you and your partner do not have a child, you can mostly do whatever you want, whenever you want. You can focus on each other and on your relationship. You devote your attention to your partner and your partner devotes his or her attention to you. When you have a child, most, if not all of your attention is devoted to your child. We have already discussed the fact that we are hardwired to protect our young—to ensure their survival. This means sacrificing sleep to ensure our newborn child is fed every several hours. This means watching a small toddler as it starts crawling and lunging at every breakable object within its reach. It means paying such close attention to this tiny human, who is completely oblivious to every sharp corner that it can and absolutely will bump into. I swear, when a baby learns to walk, it's like it is deliberately trying to bang its head on everything. This level of laser focus not only takes attention away from your partner. It leaves you too exhausted to spend quality time with him or her or, frankly, do much other than long for sweet, sweet sleep—which is now but a distant memory.

I have witnessed countless marriages fall apart when one partner feels neglected by the other. I represented a woman, let's call her Stella, who was divorcing her wife, let's call her Stephanie. Stella, who was the biological mother impregnated via sperm donor, carried and gave birth to the couple's child. When the child was born, Stella stayed home with and breastfed the child. Stephanie was the breadwinner. Her job was demanding, which meant she was not home with the baby as often as Stella was. Stephanie felt marginalized, in part because the child was not biologically hers, and in other part because she felt Stella was devoting all of her attention to the child. Stephanie felt she had been replaced and that she was no longer important to Stella. Stella still loved Stephanie. She didn't show her in the ways she had before their baby was born. Out of necessity, Stella devoted 100 percent of her attention to feeding, nurturing, and keeping their child alive.

In small part, Stella used the fact that she was the child's biological mother to aggrandize herself. The more Stella insinuated she was the more important of the two parents, the more insignificant Stephanie felt. And the more insignificant Stephanie felt, the more she tried to use her financially superior position to belittle or altogether financially dominate Stella. This back-and-forth game of one-upmanship crescendoed into an all-out battle for dominance in the relationship, until each partner ultimately viewed herself as the other's opponent.

This dynamic is pervasive in homosexual and heterosexual relationships alike, though I find it to be most prevalent in relationships where one partner—most often the husband—is a narcissist or has narcissistic tendencies. This feels like the appropriate place to remind you, I am not a psychologist or a psychiatrist. I in no way purport to diagnose personality disorders or provide counseling. I do, however, deal with narcissists on a daily basis. I have been asked to speak on podcasts on the subject of divorcing a narcissist. It's a real hot-button topic in Family Law, probably because the most bitter, acrimonious divorces and custody battles seem to involve a narcissist. In the chapter "How Many Light Bulbs Does a Narcissist Need? None, He Uses Gaslighting," we defined narcissism and talked about the ways to identify a narcissist. We also discussed why a narcissist's charm may prove it difficult to identify one.

Yet, when a child is introduced into the relationship equation, a narcissist almost always rears his ugly head. Another Family Law attorney once said to me, "The term narcissist is so overused." Respectfully, I disagree. The term isn't overused. Our line of work just lends itself to the type.

Too frequently, I represent women in divorces against male narcissists. The pattern almost always goes something like this: during the courtship period, the woman will often be drawn to the narcissist's charisma and confidence. The narcissist will make his partner feel she is a prize. The narcissist's partner reflects favorably on the narcissist. As a narcissist needs to impress and be admired, it follows that his choice in partner must impress and even be coveted by others.

The reason relationships with narcissists almost always fail when a child is introduced is apparent. A narcissist will select a partner who worships him. When the child is born, attention is taken away from the narcissist. It is more than this, though. In the case where the husband is the narcissist and the wife gives birth to the couple's child, the narcissist's physical attraction to his wife may wane as she gains weight or her appearance changes during pregnancy and after giving birth. The narcissist will perceive his wife's less attractive appearance (his words, not mine) as a poor reflection on him. If the narcissist's wife is "less attractive," then, by extension, the narcissist will not be admired by others like he was when his wife was "more attractive." This is not to say a woman is less attractive after she has given birth. She may be more attractive in so many ways. From a narcissist's purely superficial perspective, this is the case.

The narcissist might suggest that his wife get liposuction, a tummy tuck, or a boob job. Or, sensing her husband's dwindling interest in her, the wife will ask to get cosmetic procedures. The husband will encourage the wife's request instead of reassuring her that she is beautiful and dissuading her from undergoing painful and costly procedures to alter her appearance. The wife will convince herself that her husband is so supportive, when, in reality, the predominant reason the wife thinks she needs surgery is to please her husband. She feels he won't love her unless she's attractive. Whether he says it or not, she knows he is not attracted to her unless she maintains a certain standard of beauty.

All the cosmetic procedures in the world won't be enough to salvage this relationship. So long as the wife is devoting her attention to the child and not to her husband, the husband feels marginalized. The narcissist *needs* continuous adulation. Ultimately, he will seek it elsewhere. He will have an affair and feel perfectly justified in doing so. As he is incapable of accepting any responsibility for his contribution to the demise of the relationship—after all, he is perfect—he will blame the affair on his wife for forcing him to stray from the marriage. I kid you not, narcissists *always* point the finger at the wife, deflecting any responsibility for the infidelity. In the narcissist's mind, he would not have had to seek attention elsewhere if his wife hadn't stopped worshiping him.

And, since narcissists lack empathy and feel the rules do not apply to them, they do not play nice in the divorce process. The narcissist will deliberately do anything to hurt his wife in any way possible. How dare she stop idolizing him! A narcissist has been on the opposing side of some of the ugliest divorces I have litigated. The narcissist makes it his sole aim to destroy his former spouse.

In those cases that the wife dares to initiate the divorce, the narcissist will penalize his estranged wife in cruel ways, such as alienating their children or cutting off his wife's access to all finances. Ironically, when the wife initiates the divorce, the narcissist will agree to stop tormenting his estranged wife on the condition that she reconciles with him. When the narcissist initiates the divorce, he will gaslight the wife, making it his sole mission to hurt her in every conceivable way. He will use subversive ploys to force her into accepting whatever horrible and insulting offer he wants his wife to take—even if that means she has no way to support herself or the couple's child. The narcissist will use financial terrorism and any other nefarious methods to leave his wife so desperate to finalize the divorce that she will accept his deeply inequitable offer.

At the very start of my career, I represented a woman, let's call her Jane. She was divorcing a narcissist, let's call him Thomas. Although Thomas had no interest in exercising custody of their child, let's call her Rose, Thomas waged a merciless custody battle. He did this with the sole aim of hurting Jane—to punish her for leaving him. Over the course of their contentious divorce, Thomas did anything and everything to alienate Rose from Jane; to annihilate their once close mother-daughter relationship. Thomas did this to attempt to win sole physical custody of Rose. He didn't actually want sole custody, but he knew that by obtaining it he would destroy Jane. Watching the incendiary, dishonest tactics Thomas used to manipulate poor Rose revealed to me exactly the way Stockholm Syndrome works. Parental alienation is such a gradual, insidious process that by the time its effects are apparent, it is often too late to reverse the irreparable damage.

Thomas intentionally embarked on his crusade, resting only once he had succeeded in alienating Rose from Jane. When he was assured that Rose was aligned with him, he instructed her to plant drugs in Jane's home, which Rose willingly did. She was convinced that her mother didn't love her and that her father did—a complete myth heinously perpetuated by Thomas. After Rose planted the drugs, Thomas instructed Rose to "find" the drugs and call the police to report the very drugs that she had planted at Thomas's behest. When the police arrived, Rose showed the drugs to them. Jane volunteered to submit to a drug test. After all, the drugs were not hers.

Thomas didn't stop to acknowledge that, in destroying Rose's relationship with Jane, he also irremediably damaged Rose. Thomas spent months manipulatively spoon-feeding Jane awful lies about her mother. He used the fact that Jane was in a new relationship with another man to brainwash Rose into believing she was no longer important to Jane. He convinced Rose that her mother had replaced her. Thomas worked on Rose with Machiavellian prowess until Rose accepted that her mother abandoned her. Thomas didn't recognize (or maybe he didn't care about) the extreme psychological and emotional damage he caused Rose. He didn't seem bothered by the abandonment issues young Rose would carry with her throughout her life. Sweet Rose was merely a pawn in her dad's sadistic game of subterfuge. Every opportunity to convince Rose that her mother didn't love her was also an opportunity for Thomas to convince Rose that he was the sole parent who did. There exists no greater example of the narcissist's lack of empathy than a father who selfishly harms his child to satiate his own ego.

At the University of Narcissism, Parental Alienation 101 seems to be a part of the core curriculum. I have represented several mothers who were extremely close to their children (usually daughters) until the narcissistic father made a calculated effort to exert influence over the children and turn them against their mothers. For some reason, these men always have an endless stream of funds to pay attorneys (and buy gifts for their daughters), while the mothers are left spending their life's savings on attorneys to salvage their relationships with their children. It is truly devastating.

I once spoke with a psychologist who specialized in parental alienation. He recommended that the alienated child be removed from the parent who was causing the parental alienation. He further suggested that the child be placed into the sole custody of the parent from whom the child had been alienated. While this was the expert's recommendation, it is also an unrealistic one for several reasons: 1) A child who is alienated from his or her parent will, by definition, not want to be placed into that parent's sole physical custody; and 2) To remove a child from the alienating parent, the Court would have first had to have made a finding that parental alienation exists.

Yet, the perfidious nature of parental alienation, when coupled with the narcissist's charm, renders it challenging for a judge to determine with any degree of certainty that parental alienation exists. This dilemma is complicated by a number of factors. Even in the absence of parental alienation, a child may harbor resentment toward one of his or her divorcing parents. A child, particularly a teenager, may prefer to live with the more permissive parent, for obvious reasons. For example, the child will express his or her desire to live with dad, not because the child is alienated from mom, but because the child gets to do whatever he or she wants at dad's house. It may be difficult for a judge to distinguish true parental alienation from mere teenage angst. Or it could be that, in court, each parent presents such diametrically opposing, albeit equally convincing, narratives. The villain in each parent's story is always the other. The judge does not know which parent to believe. I once heard a judge say, "The truth lies somewhere in between each party's story." Judges tend to be wise. But judges make rulings based on evidence, not speculation. The fact that a child wants to spend more time with one parent than the other is not always the result of parental alienation. Judges must be cautious. At the same time, their failure to suss out real parental alienation can forever ruin the parent-child relationship.

Yes, you should definitely steer clear of narcissists. They make for really awful marital partners and even worse opponents in divorces. In the event you decide to spend your life with a narcissist, you may want to think twice before having children with him or her. Can you have a meaningful relationship with a narcissist? I suppose so. I don't really get much of a glimpse into relationships that succeed. I deal in failed relationships. I can emphatically say that a very large number of relationships that fail involve a narcissist and a child or children. And they are among the most embittered divorces.

A Child Will Not Save Your Relationship

There is an all-too-prevalent misconception about marriage and children. Many seem to think that getting married or having a child will fix a tumultuous or failing relationship. This chapter is about children, so I will not focus on marriage other than to say, getting married *never, ever*, under *no* circumstances, will save a relationship. Period. End of story.

Children will not fix a floundering relationship either. We have extensively discussed the fact that a child requires both of its parents to jointly make decisions. For the most part, this necessitates that they agree or at least engage in respectful discourse to reach a compromise. They must do this when they are sleep deprived, tired, stressed out, overwhelmed, and depleted of energy. This scenario lends itself to *more* fighting, not less.

Children do not destroy marriages. Children destroy bad marriages. It is little wonder that so many people get divorced after they have had a child or children. After many years of arguing, the resentment escalates. The constant fighting is a depressing reminder to the couple that they are trapped. Day in and day out, they are relegated to an emotionally draining situation merely to ensure that they can continue to be a part of their children's lives on a regular basis. They are no longer attracted to each other. They identify their partner as the source of their stress and misery. Living in the same household makes this exponentially daunting. This scenario is analogous to going to the grocery store, spotting someone you know and maybe dislike, and ducking out with the stealth-like precision of a ninja before he or she spots you—except, in your own home, you are constantly running into that person and being forced to make small talk in the frozen food aisle. I'm pretty sure this is what Dante contemplated when he wrote about the ninth circle of Hell.

Having children will only hold up a magnifying lens to your existing problems. You soon forget that instant when you both ogled your newborn baby, so overcome by the fact that your love for one another made a person. That single, perfect, and yes, fleeting moment, forever encapsulated on social media, disappears quicker than it took you to post about it. Reality quickly sinks in, setting the relationship on its inevitable trajectory toward divorce.

How deeply unfair to place that kind of pressure on an innocent baby. It should not be born into this world, tasked with the gargantuan responsibility of repairing your broken marriage. When I was a kid, one of my biggest fears was that my parents would get divorced. (Yes, I was a weird and slightly neurotic child.) I thought about whether I would want to live with my mom or my dad. I worried that, by choosing to live with my mom, I would hurt my dad's feelings. I also worried that, by choosing to live with my dad, I would never eat again because I wasn't quite sure my dad knew how to boil water, let alone make delicious pancakes. In hindsight, I think it strange that I tasked myself with the responsibility of deciding whether I would reside with my mom or my dad. Then again, children uniquely perceive adult situations beyond their comprehension.

I recall one specific occasion in which my parents were arguing. My mom was not speaking to my dad. I thought to myself, "This is it. So much for my cushy life. I'm not going to get to see my dad every day anymore. Will he be okay? How will he feed himself? How will he take care of me? Will my mom start dating someone new? Will I like this person? Will my dad feel sad when he sees my mom dating someone new? Will they have to sell our house? Where will my brother and I live? Will we have to go to a new school?" Such questions flooded my mind, bringing me to tears. My deliberations offer a tiny glimpse into the thought process of a child whose parents are splitting up, except my parents never actually separated.

My parents worked through their conflict. I couldn't have been more than eight or nine years old. Yet, I so vividly recall the feelings I experienced over the course of those several days. I was terrified, anxious, and unable to focus on much else. My parents may not have actually contemplated divorce. But in my child brain, I assumed the worst.

A child's home and parents represent stability. To take away the safety that this stability gives the child can be traumatic. Children are resilient and adaptable. The separation of a child's parents and shuffling between two households is disquieting for children. Relationships deteriorate. People grow apart. When, after they separate, both people remain amicable and effectively co-parent, the children are usually happy and well-adjusted. Divorce does not automatically sentence your child to a life on the therapist's couch. But ideally, you want to enter the right relationship and avoid divorce. When you know your relationship is broken, the most selfish thing you can do is have a child to save your relationship. There. I said it. After you determine that you and your partner do not share fundamental values, or that all five foundational Pillars are not in tip-top shape, you slam that "eject" button and end the relationship. You do not have a child! (Yes, I'm yelling! It's important!)

I cannot emphasize enough how very difficult it is to share custody of your child with someone you don't like or someone you downright loathe. You vehemently disagree with this person on significant child-rearing issues. Now that you're divorced, you aren't going to suddenly agree. If you did, you probably wouldn't be getting divorced. Most of my clients complain to me about what the other parent does in his or her household. The complaints run the gamut from, "He uses the wrong soap when he bathes our child," to "She feeds our child sugary snacks and fast food," to "Our child desperately needs therapy, and the other parent doesn't believe in it. He won't allow our child to participate in counseling." These gripes are on the tamer end of the spectrum.

When you fundamentally value different things, you will fundamentally disagree on how to raise your children. You will end up spending thousands of dollars on attorneys—fighting over whose way is better. By hoping that children will fix your relationship, you will end up with a broken relationship and broken children. Except, once you bring a child into the world, that child exists. That child will forever bind you to your partner and be the source of your disagreements with your him or her. Those disagreements will upset you so deeply because they pertain to your child. Your child will be acutely aware that he or she is the source of your and your partner's disagreements. In turn, your child will blame himself or herself for your divorce. It is not your child's fault that you are getting divorced. Your child will feel like it is, though. Your child will carry this guilt through the rest of his or her life. Family Law judges frequently admonish divorcing couples: "Your child knows he or she is one-half mom and one-half dad. If your child knows that mom hates dad, your child will think, 'mom hates half of me.' Or, if your child knows that dad hates mom, your child will think, 'dad hates half of me.'" Do you want your child to think that you hate a part of him or her? When you despise your former partner, your child will know it, as a result of which your child will forever be saddled with feelings of guilt, self-doubt, and even self-loathing. This will have a far-reaching, detrimental impact on your child's self-esteem, selection of romantic partner and all other aspects of your child's life—all because you were unwilling to end a relationship you *knew* you should have.

I am not trying to shame or guilt trip anyone. I am trying to scare you into seriously considering the repercussions of your decisions. Nothing about this example is hyperbolic. Sadly, I see it over and over again. While I empathize with my clients, I am utterly devastated by the heart-wrenching impact this scenario has on the child or children involved. In large part, I have written this book to try to prevent as many children as possible from going through something that no child should have to experience. I hope you're scared. You're scared, right?

Chapter 12:
If It's Broke, Don't Fix It

"The world breaks everyone, and afterward,
some are strong at the broken places."
—Ernest Hemingway

We've arrived at our next F-Word—Fixing. You can't fix anyone. If you go into a relationship thinking you can fix someone, then you might as well go ahead and fork over that retainer to me now. Can people grow? Absolutely! Can people evolve? Of course! Do people change? Not really, not unless, of course, they want to. A brilliant therapist once reminded me of this idiom: "A tiger doesn't change its stripes." To think we will fix someone who doesn't want to change is masochistic, and I'm sorry (I'm not really all that sorry), plain obtuse. Yes, the need to fix is another predictable pattern that, with almost absolute certainty, will lead to the demise of your relationship.

So many of my clients have stayed in relationships that were self-admittedly "horrible." One client in particular married a man who treated her wonderfully one day and horribly the next. She didn't know whether she would wake up to Dr. Jekyll or Mr. Hyde. She clung desperately to the hope that on these good days—which were few and far between—her husband had finally seen the light or changed. The intermittent good day became the best day ever—like an addict's first heroin fix after weeks of going without one. It somehow justified that her husband was openly having affairs or being gratuitously mean to her. She naively lived with the enduring hope that one day, the switch would simply flip, and this otherwise wonderful person's really egregious flaws would be "fixed." Of course, that never happened, and she and her husband ultimately divorced. My client's hope that she could fix her husband reminds me of one of my favorite sayings: "Wish in one hand and spit in the other. See which one fills up first." I'll give you a hint—it's not the one you wish into.

I have a friend, let's call him Wesley, who married a woman, let's call her Kendra. Kendra struggled with severe mental illness. She was on several medications that suppressed her libido and caused her to gain weight. A vicious cycle, the weight gain made Kendra even more self-conscious, contributing to her already existing insecurities and worsening her mental health issues. During their relationship, Wesley and Kendra broke up and got back together more than once. Each time, Wesley called me and shared the ways he would care for Kendra. He is such a kind human being. A few times, I pointed out to him that he was so desperately trying to fix Kendra because he was avoiding fixing something within himself. Despite agreeing with me, Wesley continued to break up and get back together with Kendra, completely ignoring what I said to him.

One day, I got a call from Wesley. You know the one. "I asked Kendra to marry me!" I couldn't muster the energy to even feign excitement. I was happy that, at that very moment, Wesley was happy. I also knew the inevitable direction this marriage was headed. I know the patterns that destine a relationship for failure. This was undeniably one of those patterns.

Over the next year, I lost contact with Wesley. Then, a year after Wesley married Kendra, I received a call. It was Wesley. He was getting divorced. He explained to me that his relationship with Kendra caused him to retreat from all his friends. Red flag much?! (That's a rhetorical question.) By convincing himself that he could fix Kendra,

Wesley justified staying in the relationship. Had he admitted he could not fix Kendra, Wesley would have had to end his relationship with her. Again, we come back to our old friend fear. Remember earlier when I told you that fear is virtually the single most reason every relationship fails? Although I am an infamous drama queen, *this time*, I wasn't being dramatic. Afraid to end the relationship and lose someone he loved, Wesley persuaded himself he could fix Kendra. By fixing her, Wesley could remain in the relationship and didn't have to be alone.

One of the biggest mistakes people make is to stay in a relationship just because they love their partner. There has to be more. There are so many wonderful people whom I love dearly. It does not mean they would all make good life partners for me. Needless to say, when Wesley separated from Kendra, he was devastated. He was a complete wreck. This divorce was inevitable, yet totally avoidable. I hope Wesley's pain served its pedagogic function—no, *not* to always listen to me, but to teach him that a fulfilling and long-lasting relationship is one in which his partner is his teammate, not a project.

By devoting himself to fixing Kendra, Wesley sent the resounding message that Kendra was broken. This reinforced Kendra's self-esteem issues and solidified the imbalance in the relationship dynamic. Wesley promoted himself to caretaker, unconsciously assuring Kendra's dependency on him. Wesley didn't do this solely to avoid fixing his own problems. He also did it to feel needed. Feeling needed filled some sort of void within him. Wesley and Kendra were not a team. He was like a basketball player trying to dunk while carrying his wounded teammate on his back. This makes it difficult to jump.

Think you can fix your partner? Wish in one hand and spit in the other. See which one fills up first. Spoiler alert: it's the one you spit in.

It's Only Downhill from Here

It's no secret. As our relationship progresses, we are less concerned with impressing our partner. We feel comfortable being ourselves. Comfort should not be mistaken for complacency. The former can be quite wonderful. The latter can and will lead to problems in the relationship. A complacent person is one who takes his or her partner for granted. This person may stop showing any physical or even emotional interest in his or her partner. This person may stop showing his or her partner appreciation. Complacency is exhibited through indifference. A woman, who previously felt the self-conscious need to always wear makeup around her partner, may now feel comfortable enough to be around her partner without makeup on. In large part, this is attributable to the fact that her partner has made her feel beautiful regardless of whether she wears makeup. This woman has not become complacent because she stopped wearing makeup around her partner. She continues to show her partner how much she appreciates him or her. This woman is now comfortable being her authentic self around her partner.

As your comfort grows, you no longer make it your sole aim to impress your partner. Your partner is already impressed by you. He or she already knows how impressive you are. Your partner doesn't care about your morning breath or how you look without makeup on. He or she loves you and all of your imperfections. Your partner so values your qualities and achievements that he or she doesn't believe there is anyone better suited for him or her.

Now that your partner is no longer trying to impress you and you are no longer trying to impress your partner, why do you think your partner will suddenly fix all of those things about himself or herself you want to change? I don't mean superficial things, like the way it drives you crazy when your partner scrapes his fork against his front teeth when he takes a bite of his food. I mean things like, at social functions, your partner routinely says the most inappropriate things, embarrassing you in front of friends, colleagues, and family. You have spoken to your partner about this. Your partner promised not to do this. Without fail, your partner still does it. He or she cannot control it. You have to make excuses for all the reasons your partner cannot attend work functions. You've tried to fix it. You keep hoping your partner will figure it out. Reality check—things will only get worse.

The expectation that as the relationship progresses you will magically mold your partner into your ideal version of them is unreasonable. You can fix a car. You can fix a house. You cannot fix a person. So, stop trying!

As a relationship develops, people let down their guard. So why would your partner improve his or her behavior over time? If anything, your partner will care less about impressing you, and he or she will act worse.

Chapter 13:
Two Wrongs Make a Fight

"The wound is where the light enters."
—Rumi

We are not always looking to fix our partner, though. Sometimes, we use the fact that *we* are broken to justify being with another who, too, is broken.

In what is an all-too-familiar scenario, a man, let's call him Matt, hasn't spoken to his mother in ten years. Matt would love to speak to his mother. His mother refuses to speak to him. As a result, Matt has abandonment issues. He feels unlovable and even undeserving of love.

Matt's partner, let's call him Mike, does not speak to his dad. When Mike was five years old, Mike's dad cheated on Mike's mom. Mike has trust issues. He has a deep distrust of all men.

When Matt and Mike met, they believed they had so much in common. OMG, their first names both start with the letter "M" and they both love paddle boarding and kombucha! It's destiny! Right?

It plays out something like this: Matt, who is abandoned by his own mother—the woman who is supposed to unconditionally love him—believes he is unlovable and, therefore, unworthy of love. When somebody does love him, this someone's qualities and values are largely irrelevant to Matt. The love is so powerful, Matt is willing to overlook everything else. The love of another fills the void within him left by his mother. As Matt struggles with abandonment issues, he clings desperately to the person he loves, vowing never to let go, no matter how wrong for him this person may be. He thinks it better to have the love of the wrong person than no person at all, and consequently, selects the wrong person.

Mike, scarred by his dad's infidelity, believes all men cheat and will ultimately leave. His father walked out on the family when he was five, and he has not known the love of a father. So, when Matt comes around and offers Mike a love he knows Matt will never take away—the love of a man that fills the void left by Mike's father—Mike seeks comfort in that love.

It does not matter that Mike wants children and Matt does not. It does not matter that Mike wants to travel the world and Matt prefers to stay home. He has never left the city he grew up in and he has no desire to do so. It does not matter that, politically, Mike is ultra-liberal and Matt is a staunch conservative. Neither one of them cares . . . at least not right now. Neither one of them stops to consider the ways their diametrically opposed fundamental values will almost certainly lead to the demise of their relationship in the long run. Each assuages the other's fears.

Matt and Mike are like two halves of a broken glass glued together. Had you poured water into this glass, the water would seep out through the cracks. If you held this glass, it would fall apart in your hand.

Matt's answer is not to find just any partner who will love him. Matt's solution is to work through his fears of abandonment. He must recognize that he is deserving of love so he can find a mate with whom he is compatible. The fact that Mike loves Matt, alone, does not render Mike the right life partner for Matt. Mike's answer is not to find a partner who has abandonment issues. Mike's solution is to work on his trust issues. Mike must come to the realization that not every man is his father. Not every man is unfaithful and dishonest. Mike must also understand that his father walked out on his mother. Mike's father did not walk out on Mike. Mike's father did not love Mike any less when he left Mike's mother, even if Mike interpreted it this way. The moment Mike understands that not every man is dishonest, he will stop seeking a partner for the wrong reasons and choose one for the right reasons.

To an extent, we have already addressed this in the context of the Communication Pillar. Our past determines our understanding of love, and in turn, the type of love we seek. Our behavior in relationships is shaped by our past experiences and traumas. We form relationships for the wrong reasons only to play out our dysfunctions in those relationships. Before you allow your past experiences and traumas to select your life partner, you must fix yourself, so that *you* select your life partner. Your common ground with your partner cannot be your mutual problems. While two people who have gone through similar traumatic experiences are certainly in a better position to understand one another, their shared traumas should not be the reason they are together. Their shared pain is misconstrued as a shared fundamental value, overshadowing each person's true fundamental values. They bond over their collective traumas without addressing the ways those traumas adversely impact them.

If you want to find a meaningful relationship, you must first turn the mirror on yourself. Reflect upon what you see. Ask yourself—am I mentally and emotionally healthy enough to be a good teammate and partner to another? This is no easy task. It presupposes that you, yourself, are ready and able to recognize that you may need fixing. It requires you to be willing to be alone, or at the very least, to avoid a relationship until you face your emotional and psychological scars. You must do the difficult, uncomfortable, and painful work to recognize the origin of your wounds and heal them. To quote the great RuPaul, "If you can't love yourself, how in the hell are you gonna love somebody else?"

Wounds heal. Scars remain forever. There is not a person among us without scars. In a beautiful way, they make us human. They make us vulnerable. Our scars are an integral part of the complexity of our makeup. The question becomes, do we allow our scars to dictate our choices, or do we take charge of our scars, using them as opportunities for personal growth? Do we become the victims of our circumstances, or do we triumph over them?

In Japan, the art of repairing broken pottery is known as Kintsugi. According to this philosophy, broken pottery is pieced back together using a mix of lacquer dusted or mixed with powdered gold. When the broken pottery is fixed, the gold lines are visible in the places where the pottery shattered. Kintsugi is predicated on the belief that breakage and repair are part of the history of the object, rather than something to be disguised. You are not a victim of your breakage. Your scars do not get to make decisions for you. *You* get to make decisions for you. Your scars are part of your intricate history. They do not define you. They do not destroy you. You pick up the pieces, glue yourself back together and flaunt those exquisite golden lines that make you who you are. Despite your past, you deserve to be in a meaningful relationship. You need to take the time to mend the cracks.

Chapter 14:
And They Lived Happily Never After

> "Life isn't a fairy tale. If you lose a
> shoe at midnight, you're drunk."
> —Darynda Jones

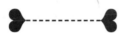

Extra! Extra! Read all about it. Your wedding is not the most important day of your life. Wait, what?! I look stunning in that off-white taffeta Monique Lhuillier ballgown. That sweetheart top really lifts and separates just right. Buuuuuuut, we've already paid the deposit on the swans. The band does the best version of Justin Timberlake's "SexyBack" that's sure to blow people's minds on the dance floor!

Allow me to break it to you not so gently: your wedding day is probably the *least* important day of your entire life—maybe not in your mind, but, like, on planet Earth.

Yes, dear reader, we have arrived at our fifth F-Word—Fairy Tale. The Merriam-Webster dictionary defines "fairy tale" as a "made up story usually designed to mislead." MISLEAD. They lied to you . . . intentionally. Yes, you drank the Kool-Aid—and now it's time to spit it out.

In our society, we romanticize courtship and marriage. We have grown up in the cult of Disney. From a young age, we are indoctrinated with the belief that the wedding is followed by the "happily ever after." We convince ourselves, "If I can make it to that wedding, everything will be peachy."

Cinderella saunters down the palace steps, adorned in a white, floor-length gown that highlights her fourteen-inch waistline. Her veil, which is held at each end by two picturesque bluebirds, impeccably flutters behind her, as she is ushered into a gold-encrusted horse-drawn carriage, lined in red taffeta, no less. We are told this is "The End." We naively accept that Cinderella and Prince Charming live "happily ever after." We delusionally come to equate marriage with "happily ever after," as though, despite the problems in our relationship, marriage will miraculously fix them. It doesn't! As Merriam-Webster so bluntly reminds us, this story is actually written to mislead us into accepting something that isn't true. In a court of law, that would be called fraud—and would carry with it a verdict for substantial punitive damages.

We are taught that the pinnacle of our lives is our wedding day, without any glimpse into what the "ever after" part actually looks like. It's not Disney's (or the Brothers Grimm's) fault. Cinderella is a feel-good story, with a happy ending. It's *your* fault. You buy the promises advertised to you, failing to distinguish fantasy from reality. In real life, your wedding day is not "the end." It is merely the beginning. There is an entire lifetime that follows—replete with obstacles, uncertainties, and difficulties.

To say "they lived happily ever" is to irresponsibly overlook an integral part of the story. Disney never dared peel back the curtain. You didn't see Cinderella exhausted and disheveled after a day of chasing two children, passed out on the couch at eight o'clock, too tired to be intimate with her husband. You never saw Prince Charming sitting on the couch in sweats—you know, the pair with that giant hole in the inseam—scratching his balls and burping, while Cinderella (who has packed on a few pounds since the "big day") sits next to him in an old T-shirt covered in spaghetti stains. You never saw Cinderella and

Prince Charming at each other's throats after Prince Charming was laid off with no way to make next month's mortgage payment. Prince Charming, by virtue of who he is, cannot be laid off, and most likely doesn't need to work or have a mortgage. So, in what world can you base your life on this unrealistic allegory?

I am not telling you anything you don't already know. I am reminding you that a meaningful relationship is one in which you and your partner still make each other happy fifty years from now. When you and your partner value very different things, when you want different things in life, when you are not compatible on a deeper level, you won't make each other happy. You probably won't make it fifty years.

Friedrich Nietzsche said: "If you know the why, you can live any how." What poignant insight into the human psyche. Someone who aimlessly wades through the dating pool will likely gravitate toward the first superficially appealing person that floats by. They will waste their time, investing their energy into people who are wrong for them, because they did not take the time to identify their fundamental values and conduct the job interview. Conversely, when you define *why* you want something, you expend your energy on *how* to find it. You won't indiscriminately meander through the dating pool. You will vigorously swim directly toward an identifiable destination, swatting off any hogwash that hinders you from reaching it. Until you define the reasons certain qualities, characteristics, and fundamental values are important to you, you will haphazardly traipse the dating field, persuading yourself some random hot guy or girl you met on that app is your "soulmate." (P.S. He or she isn't. Swipe left.)

Identifying your fundamental values *is* the "why." When you are a person who fundamentally values adventure, you must find a partner who also values adventure. Why? You believe that no matter what your age, you will always crave new experiences. Your treasure trove consists of memories of travel to exotic destinations, cage-diving with great white sharks in South Africa, climbing Mt. Kilimanjaro, dining in a snow castle in Finland (the tables were made of actual ice!), and microlighting over the Victoria Falls. The reason you have defined adventure as one of your top fundamental values is that it makes you feel fulfilled. Without new experiences—in whatever form they may take—life isn't worth living. Your "why" is "adventure fulfills me." Your "how" then becomes to find a partner who craves and is equally fulfilled by adventure.

This is a good place to pause and tackle our final exercise.

Exercise 6: Finding My "Why"

In defining your fundamental values, you first thought in broad terms, establishing what is currently important to you. This was intended to get you to start thinking about what you value, not necessarily what you fundamentally value.

Next, you dug a little deeper. You distinguished your fleeting interests from your core beliefs, to define your *fundamental* values. You came up with three to five values that are so inextricable to your being that they represent who you are.

Now, I want you to think about *why* each value you identified is so fundamental to you. As we have concluded, when you know your why, you can find any how. Understanding the reason a value is so essential to you allows you to understand the reason your life partner must share that value. In turn, you will deliberately search for a life partner who values what you value, for the same reason you covet those values.

In each space below, write down each value you have identified as fundamental to you. Then, write the reason—your *why*—each fundamental value is so important to you.

Fundamental Value: _____
Reason(s) You Fundamentally Value It:

_____

_____

_____

_____

_____

_____

_____

Fundamental Value: _____
Reason(s) You Fundamentally Value It:

_____

_____

_____

_____

_____

_____

_____

Fundamental Value: _____
Reason(s) You Fundamentally Value It:

_____

_____

_____

_____

_____

_____

_____

Fundamental Value: _____

Reason(s) You Fundamentally Value It:

_____

_____

_____

_____

_____

_____

Fundamental Value: _____

Reason(s) You Fundamentally Value It:

_____

_____

_____

_____

_____

_____

Look at your answers. The purpose of this exercise is to recognize the underlying reason or reasons each fundamental value is so important to you. When you know what you want and the reason you want it, you are far more likely to figure out how to get it. Remember, something that seems like a fundamental value may be a superficial manifestation of some deeper need. In the example I gave earlier, two people may love to travel and travel frequently when they are young and relatively free of responsibilities. However, once they pursue serious careers and have children, they are unable to travel with the same frequency and as capriciously as they once did. The desire to fervently travel was merely a manifestation of the actual fundamental value—the need for adventure.

In identifying why adventure was so fundamental to their lives, they searched for a partner for whom adventure fulfilled the same needs. The job interview was geared at ascertaining whether the other person craved adventure for similar reasons.

On the contrary, when your "why" for staying in a relationship or getting married is the wedding, your "how" will be, "How do I get married?" or "How do I get to the wedding?" Your thought process is not, "How do I pick the person who is *right* for me for the rest of my life?" Rather, it is, "How do I pick *a* person?" When the proposal or your wedding day are your "why," the "job interview" process will be inconsequential—after all, anyone willing to marry you will fit the position. You will neglect to consider whether you and your partner share fundamental values. You will not invest the requisite time and care to build a solid foundation. You will convince yourself that this person is "Mr. or Ms. Right" or "the one." They happen to be in the right place at the right time. You have fun together. You are the age at which all of your friends are getting married. If you break up with your partner now, you will have to start over, and God forbid, as you inch closer to thirty-five, the thought is far too unbearable.

Now, let's imagine this: your "why" is to have a meaningful and happy life. Your "why" is to find a partner who will push you to be the best version of yourself, as opposed to someone who "completes" you. You are complete on your own. Your partner should not complete you. He or she should *enhance* how wonderful and amazing you already are. Your "why" is to find a partner who fundamentally values the same things as you. You understand the reason you fundamentally value certain things. You also understand the reason it is so important you and your partner share fundamental values.

You may or may not want a wedding. If you do want a wedding, you see the wedding as more of a celebration to be shared with your friends and family, as opposed to the opportunity to be a bridezilla . . . ahem, princess for a day. It is not about the tablecloths that are the perfect hue of blush, or the fact that your bouquet has pink peonies in it. Guess what? Tomorrow, you will wake up with half of that fake eyelash dangling off your eyelid and that long-lasting mauve lipstick smeared across your chin, and you will be married 'til death do you part. Sure, you will relive your glory day through the photos you get back in three to five weeks. You'll post them on every social media account you have—hashtag "bestdayever" and "blessed." If that was truly the "best day ever," then no day for the rest of your entire life can top it. What a sad life when you peak at thirty-one or twenty-nine or whatever age you happen to get married at.

So, your "why" must be to find someone with whom you share at least three to five fundamental values and someone with whom you have built a solid foundation. You work together so well as a team, supporting each other through the lows, and cheering each other on through life's obstacles. You communicate effectively to build a deeper understanding of one another's needs and navigate disagreements. You respect your partner enough to still regard his or her thoughts, even when they diverge from your own. It follows, then, that your "how" will be geared toward doing whatever necessary to find *that*. You will approach dating more critically, rejecting a potential partner who doesn't meet your criteria, even if, OMG! you both have dogs and love long bike rides on the beach.

Chapter 15:
Meet the Family

"The other night, I ate at a real nice family
restaurant. Every table had an argument going."
—George Carlin

Meeting the family is a big step in any relationship. It's a big deal for the family. It's a big deal for the person introducing his or her significant other to the family. It's a big deal for the person being introduced to the family.

For many, it is a make-it-or-break-it step. Family is also our final F-Word. In my experience, serious acrimony between your partner and your family or you and your partner's family is a sure recipe for failure. Although there is no right time to introduce your partner to your family, from my perspective, making the introduction earlier is preferable to making it later.[2] Your family knows you better than almost anyone. With exception, of course, they want what is best for you. They want you to be happy. You are intoxicated with infatuation. They are the designated driver—in a superior position to offer an objective opinion. Ask for it. Value it. They may say things you don't want to hear. Be open to listening. During the course of a divorce, I often hear clients tell me that at the end of the relationship, they came to realize what their families had been saying all along. Personally, I think my clients

---

2 Some may not be close to their families. Others may have lost close family members, in which case, other relatives and friends may hold just as much importance in your life. These relatives and friends are interchangeable for family for the purpose of our discussion of family.

knew their families were right, but refused to admit it to themselves. One will choose to ignore the admonition of his or her family just to avoid the inevitable breakup that must follow it. One would rather grow estranged from his or her family than heed an admonition he or she innately knows to be true.

I once represented a woman, let's call her Angelica, whose family was from Northern England. Her husband, let's call him Niles, was from London. Niles's family had always disapproved of Angelica because she was from Northern England. They were classist and often made fun of her accent. They told Angelica she "wasn't good enough" for their son. This, of course, caused Angelica to feel worthless. Niles was extremely close to his family. Angelica's relationship failed for many reasons. The strain Niles's family placed on the marriage played a large part in its demise. Niles was so bonded with his family and so valued his family's opinions that he could not reconcile the conflict between his parents and his wife. He wanted to please his parents. He also wanted to please Angelica. Niles could not do both, as pleasing one automatically meant displeasing the other. The situation was exacerbated by the fact that Niles's parents constantly disparaged Angelica. She always felt insecure and inadequate; questioning whether Niles shared his parents' views of her. Every time something happened in their lives, Niles would tell his parents. He did so not with any malice, but to seek their love and support during difficult times. His parents used any misfortune as ammunition to berate Angelica, driving a deeper chasm between her and Niles.

This divorce could have been avoided had Angelica acknowledged and accepted the signs that were there all along. Niles's family had always made fun of Angelica's accent. His family always belittled her. Angelica foolishly thought, or at least hoped, that marriage would change things. It didn't. No matter how much Angelica loved Niles and wanted to spend her life with him, her first meeting with his parents (or her second or third) should have prompted her to end the relationship. Instead, she ignored the signs, hoping that, by shutting her eyes, everything would turn out okay. Many thousands of dollars spent on attorneys' fees later, and after much contentious litigation (no doubt, in large part promulgated and even funded by Niles's family), Angelica was left in a far worse position than she would have been had she acknowledged the red flags.

Niles's family was unrelenting. Angelica knew this from the very first time she met them. She hoped that once she and Niles married, Niles's family would welcome her as one of their own. They did not. Angelica again hoped Niles's parents would accept her once Angelica had children. They did not. Angelica's naive optimism ironically became the source of her deepest angst. Every dashed hope fueled Angelica's hopelessness. Søren Kierkegaard said: "There are two ways to be fooled. One is to believe what isn't true; the other is to refuse to believe what is true." By refusing to believe what she knew to be true, Angelica continued to delude herself, wishing for a different outcome. In doing so, Angelica invited the very rejection she sought to avoid. Angelica and Niles adeptly illustrate the due weight one's family must be given in a relationship.

Just as important as it is for your partner to meet your family, it is equally important for you to meet your partner's family. Through this meeting, you will learn a lot about your partner's fundamental values. Quite often, we share some, if not all, of the same fundamental values as our family. Is your partner warm and connected to his or her family? Is he or she embarrassed by them? Does your partner pick fights with his or her family? For what reason? What does your partner's family seem to fundamentally value and are these values shared by your partner? Is your partner an only child or does he or she have siblings? How does he or she relate to those siblings? Are your partner and his or her siblings close or estranged and, if so, what are the reasons? Answers to these and other questions offer invaluable insight. They provide otherwise inaccessible information to the job interview puzzle.

Your partner may tell you he or she disavows his or her family's beliefs or traditions. This may not be the case if your partner actually seeks his or her family's approval. What does your partner's family believe? Does your partner want his or her family's approval or does he or she reject it? One's actions and one's words do not always align. Observe what your partner says and what he or she does.

Often, we are so bewitched by the implications of this big step that we miss the meaningful opportunity it offers. Yes, it's exciting that your partner is ready to introduce you to his or her family. It insinuates a level of commitment that is certainly thrilling. You should be far more thrilled to be given front row, VIP access to top secret intel, which is otherwise unavailable to you—information that may be critical to whether you remain in or leave the relationship.

When your partner is close to his or her family, the family will likely play a big role in your lives. Do you like your partner's family enough to tolerate their involvement? Do you absolutely adore your partner's family? Will you enjoy their presence or dread it? If your partner is not close to his or her family, what is the reason? Does the reason cause your partner to experience internal conflict or turmoil in a way that will impact your relationship?

Ordinarily, when we have a strained relationship with our mom or dad (or both), we will choose a partner who is similar to them. We do this subconsciously, to work out the issues in our relationship with our mom or dad. We gravitate toward a recognizable dynamic because it is familiar. For instance, I represented a client whose parents divorced when she was younger. After her parents divorced, she stopped speaking to her father. This woman married (and, eventually, went on to divorce) a man who was very much like her father. This woman's relationship with her husband was like her father's relationship with her mother. She grew up watching the way her parents interacted, learning to mimic the mechanics of her parents' relationship. She went on to select a partner who was similar to her father. She proceeded to act exactly like her mother—replicating the same dysfunctional patterns. This woman's relationship with her partner became a mirror image of her parents' relationship. Meanwhile, my client's husband was so much like her father, she attempted to work out her own issues with her father by trying to change her husband. Of course, this did not end well.

In this scenario, the wife and the husband were both equally responsible for the demise of the relationship. The wife should have first addressed her issues with her father so that she could begin a relationship in a healthier way. By learning about the wife's strained relationship with her father, the husband should have paused to question the way the wife's unresolved issues with her father might impact the relationship. Undeniably, this would have required both partners to possess an acute level of self-awareness. I believe the wife and possibly even the husband did contemplate these issues prior to their marriage. I suspect they deliberately ignored these thoughts, suppressing them in favor of companionship.

Although somewhat tangential to the issue of family, this scenario warrants further exploration—insofar as it offers a glimpse into the impact dysfunctional relationships have on children. Children learn about interpersonal and romantic relationships by observing the interactions between their parents. The love shown by parents to their children teaches children how to love and be loved. The love parents show or don't show to each other also teaches children how to treat others. One of the myriad reasons we strive for a healthy relationship is to set an example for our children. They learn by mimicking what we do and say. There is no greater illustration of this than when my two-year-old son stubbed his toe and blurted out, "Oh! What the fuck!" (I have no idea where he heard this . . . I swear.)

In the case of my client, she married a man who was exactly like her father. Even as an adult, she proceeded to act toward her husband the same way her mother had acted toward her father. Her parents served as her exemplars. She followed suit.

Our families shape us. Our disfunctions, our positive and negative qualities, our anxieties, our traumas, and our beliefs are largely a product of our parents and childhood influences. Our parents teach us how to love and be loved. This is in large part the reason that children who are abused may grow up to be abusive adults. Our parents are an integral part of our development. Good or bad, they mold the way we give and receive love. Whether your partner has a relationship with his or her parent, parents, parent figures and siblings is an indispensable piece of the puzzle, warranting serious exploration. You cannot truly know a person unless you know about the influences that shaped him or her. No matter how amazing you think your partner is, no matter how much you adore him or her, you must learn about his or her family. If possible, you must meet your partner's family.

Chapter 16:
How [Insert Your Name Here]
Got Their Groove Back

"What's past is prologue."
—William Shakespeare

The decisions you make *today* exclusively determine the quality of the rest of your life. Sound ominous? Good. It should.

You now know the reasons relationships and marriages fail. Equipped with this invaluable information, you are now in the keen position to recognize and avoid certain patterns when they manifest—that is, provided you approach the dating process with the requisite objectivity.

Although I have somewhat exhaustively analyzed and dissected the patterns characteristic of virtually all failed marriages, I will distill this information into a simple checklist—one to which you may easily refer as you embark upon your journey to find the *right* life partner:

- Define your fundamental values.
- Interview the job candidate to ascertain whether he or she shares your fundamental values. Remember to distinguish fleeting interests from *fundamental* values.
- Butterflies are the enemy. Approach the most important decision you will ever make in your life rationally.
- Fear does not make decisions for you. You make decisions for yourself. Are you getting involved with this person out of fear? Are you afraid to leave a relationship because you fear you may not find

someone better? Trust your intuition. Use your intelligence to make choices. Fear does not care about the you of the future. It is not to be trusted.

- Are you trying to fix your partner? Do you need to fix yourself before you can enter a relationship in a healthy way?
- Are all the Five Pillars of your foundation intact, or will your relationship topple over?
- Do you trust your partner?
- Is your partner honest with you, and can you be honest with your partner?
- How effectively do you and your partner communicate to resolve problems? Remember, every relationship encounters bumps along the road. A successful, long-lasting relationship is defined by how efficaciously you and your partner communicate to resolve your issues.
- Do you respect your partner? Do you admire his or her qualities or achievements?
- Do you know your "why"; your reasons for being in this relationship? Is it a fairy-tale wedding? Is your impetus for committing to this person the fear of solitude?
- Have you met your partner's family? Has your partner met your family? What kind of relationship does your partner have with his or her family? What kind of relationship do you have with yours? How do your relationships with your respective families impact each of you individually, and how do they impact your relationship? Does your family like your partner? Do you like your partner's family? Does your partner's family like you? Where do you and your partner plan to live?

The next forty, sixty, or even eighty years of your life are blank pages. You are the scribe. Without devoting the necessary time to understand what you seek in your life partner, you will aimlessly meander, lost in the empty pages, relegated to repeating predictable but avoidable patterns. You will become another cliché—a statistic. Alternatively, you approach dating with purpose. You define your "why," which empowers you to find your "how." You take charge of your narrative.

I want you to shape your destiny—one that does not include you sitting at my desk, wondering where you will live or how you will feed your children. Those savings you have accumulated since your child was born should be used to send *your* child to college, not mine. I want nothing more than to shield you from the inevitable pain, the financial devastation, and the enduring scar divorce will leave on your heart and wallet alike. I want to protect your son and daughter from spending the rest of their lives blaming themselves for mommy and daddy's divorce or repeating the dysfunctional patterns in their mommy and daddy's relationship.

If only I could have stopped the sobbing forty-six-year-old mother of three from marrying her husband because she so badly wanted to be a princess for a day. If only I could have urged that man to trust his gut when his girlfriend told him she was "on birth control." If only I could have been on that first and second date to ask, "Are you close to your family?" instead of "What type of music do you like?" If only I had gotten to these people before they said "yes" to a third date, and then a fourth—before they got so emotionally invested that they were afraid to jump ship. If only they could have identified the patterns before they signed that lease on an apartment or bought their first sofa together. If only they recognized that they did not share fundamental values before they adopted a puppy.

One of my favorite poems, "The Road Not Taken" by Robert Frost, begins: "Two roads diverged in a yellow wood, / And sorry I could not travel both / And be one traveler, long I stood / And looked down one as far as I could / To where it bent in the undergrowth…" At the start of the poem, the speaker is faced with two choices. He must decide which of two roads to take. The poem ends: "Somewhere ages and ages hence: / Two roads diverged in a wood, and I— / I took the one less traveled by, / And that has made all the difference." The speaker embarks upon one path with the understanding that the choice he makes will shape his journey. Many years later, in reflecting upon the path he chose, the speaker ultimately recognizes his decision determined the outcome of his life. Our choices today decide our tomorrow.

Right now, you stand at a fork in the road. The path you take will determine whether you find a meaningful relationship or end up divorced. The road you choose makes all the difference. You don't need me to hold your hand while you cross the street. You know the patterns. You know the questions to ask. You have the tools to find a meaningful and fulfilling lifelong relationship with a true life partner. No, my office does not make its way into *your* narrative.

You possess an intelligence that bestows upon you the power to "choose between"; to choose happiness over fear, to choose the *right* partner for the *right* reasons. Your relationship will succeed because you have chosen not to fail. It all starts with a choice.

This book *is* bad for business. You know what, though? I'm perfectly all right with that.

Acknowledgments

Much like finding a meaningful relationship, writing a book is a journey. The incredible encouragement, support, and guidance I received along the way served as my trusty compass, without which I would never have arrived at my final destination.

I am so grateful to my dear unicorn friend, Kelly Kruger Brooks, for taking the time out of her busy schedule to write such a heartfelt Introduction. I can't thank you enough for your honesty and vulnerability. I still can't believe you welcomed my crazy proposition with such enthusiasm.

To the wonderful Caitlin Crosby—badass boss lady and one of the sweetest human beings anyone will ever meet: thank you for your kind words and invaluable perspective. I hope this is the first of many collaborations. You are a gem of a human being.

I remain deeply humbled by Dr. Sarah Salzman's excitement for this project and the time she devoted to it. Her expertise lends credence to my words and, let's face it, who doesn't love a little validation every now and again? In all seriousness, it feels amazing to know that someone with your caliber of knowledge and experience endorses this book. Thank you, thank you, thank you.

To my agent, Coleen O'Shea, I would have been completely lost without you. You have been and continue to be my North Star. I cannot thank you enough for the direction and advice you have offered along this surreal adventure.

I am extremely thankful to my publisher, Skyhorse, for believing in my work and, specifically, my editor, Nicole Frail, for your always insightful thoughts. Although I am (borderline psychotically) perfectionistic about my writing, your notes consistently elevate it.

This book would not have been possible without all of my wonderful clients. Thank you to each and every one of you for sharing the intimate details of your life with me, so that I could gain a deeper understanding of the innerworkings of relationships. I truly value that you entrusted me during one of the most difficult periods in your life. I hope that you learned from me as much as I learned from you. May you never need my services again!

In the first grade, I was tasked with my first ever writing assignment. I was given a set of vocabulary words and instructed to write a story using them. My mom sat with me and helped me concoct a brilliant masterpiece. (Okay, I was six years old, and it wasn't exactly James Joyce, but it was good.) From that point on, up until I graduated from high school, my mom sat with me and helped me write every essay, often, late at night (and my mom likes to go to bed early). My mom proofread my revisions. She made suggestions that cultivated my love for writing and shaped my skills as a writer. Each summer, she expected me to read at least several books and urged me to keep a list of words I didn't know, building my vocabulary. Although, as an English major, my English teachers and professors fine-tuned my writing in unimaginable ways, I attribute my passion for writing solely to my mom. This book would have certainly been far less coherent if it was not for her devotion.

I am also eternally grateful to my family and friends for your ongoing support and encouragement. I am sorry I bailed on plans to write. I love you for understanding. I swear, none of the anecdotes in this book are based on you or your relationships.

And as the music cues me to end my protracted speech and leave the stage, I must lastly, but no less importantly, thank my husband,

Joel Warsh. Not only has he shown me what a healthy and meaning-ful relationship entails, but he has been my biggest cheerleader. For over five years, he stood on the sidelines, waiving his proverbial pom-poms. (Maybe one day, he'll get real ones.) He nudged me to write and finish this book. He cared for our child so that I had the time to write and finish this book. He connected me with all of the wonderful players who would ultimately make this unfathomable dream a reality. Ordinarily, I wouldn't tarnish my reputation as a cold, heartless wife by writing something so sappy for all to see. But this seems like the appropriate time to thank you for being the best partner and teammate I could ask for. (Shhhh. Don't tell anyone I said that.)

About the Author

© Joanna DeGeneres

S arah Intelligator is a divorce attorney in Los Angeles. She earned a Juris Doctorate from Southwestern Law School. She graduated from UCLA, cum laude, with a Bachelor of Arts in English.

Practicing Family Law since 2008, Sarah has also been a yoga instructor since 2000. She organically bridged her two worlds, coining the term: "Holistic Divorce and Family Law." In helping others through their divorces, Sarah realized that she could help them avoid divorce altogether.

In her spare time, Sarah enjoys traveling and spending time with her son, Eli, and husband, Joel. She also dabbles in interior design.